BEYOND *this* DAY

THE WAY OF HOPE

*This Keepsake and Tribute is
Presented in Loving Memory of*

_____

With Sympathy by

_____

_____

_____

Date

BEYOND this DAY

THE WAY OF HOPE

A Keepsake and Tribute to Your Loved One

*Dedicated to all those
who have walked with Sorrow
and passed her lessons on.*

CONCEPT	TEXT	DESIGN
Sean Gallagher	John Sydney Tighe	Mike Lore

ShutterStock.com Photo Credits:
Eivaisla, Peter Wollinga, Jasmine_K, Smileus, Andrew F. Kazmierski, yspbqh14, prapass, biletskiy, Stephen Moehle, Kang Khoon Seang, Francesco Ferrarini, EdwinM, Seqoya, Colin D. Young, Andrew Mayovskyy, hawkeye978, Benjamin Haas, Vietnam Stock Images, Ozerov Alexander, SuriyaPhoto, NadzeyaShanchuk, Phillip Maguire, Creative Travel Projects, Aimee M Lee, Jon Bilous, badahos, isarescheewin, S.Borisov, littlenySTOCK, Dave Allen Photography, OHishiapply, Clayton Townsend, Dean Fikar, anthony heflin, Tomas Nevesely, Jorge Moro, UBC Stock, elena moiseeva, Kelly vanDellen, Aleksey Stemmer.

©2018 Good Will Publishers, Inc. All rights reserved.
Printed by Asia Printing Co., Ltd. Seoul, Korea
This book, or any part thereof, may not be reproduced in any form without written permission of the publisher.

BEYOND this DAY
THE WAY OF HOPE

PART ONE
Remembering
The Record of a Family... The Memory of a Life
9

PART TWO
A Time to Mourn
Walking with the Sorrow... Living with the Grief
29

PART THREE
Seasons of Feeling
The Movement of a Year... The Movement of a Heart
63

PART FOUR
The Way of Hope
Helpful Connections... Helpful Bereavement Resources
101

THE PURPOSE AND USE OF THIS BOOK

This volume is designed as a tribute, a keepsake and a help. It is a tribute to your recently deceased loved one, a document of your love and remembrance for someone special. It is a keepsake in which you are invited to record family history through a family chart and through selected journal entries relating to your life with your loved one and others. It is meant to be a help in that it is hoped you will find in these pages a reminder that you are not alone in your pain. In a way this book is a celebration of our human connectedness, an homage to sacrifice, commitment and love.

You may choose to use *Beyond This Day* in different ways at different times, just as we all experience our grief in our own special way and in our own time. However you choose to use your volume, it is meant to focus on the fact that our memories are a natural part of who we are and can therefore help us through difficult times. It is the sincere desire of the author, the publisher and the donors of this gift volume to touch your heart in a time when so many of us feel so alone. We hope this keepsake tribute will help you celebrate a particular life, as well as life itself. We believe you are worth the time and the energy it takes to say, "Hang in there, friend, you are in our thoughts."

May all our lives serve as tributes to those who have passed before us, ever recalling the love that was shared so that we, in turn, may pass that love on to all those near and dear to us.

"Let tears flow of their own accord: their flowing is not inconsistent with inward peace and harmony."

–Seneca

PART ONE
REMEMBERING

*"What we have once enjoyed we can never lose.
All that we love deeply becomes a part of us."*
-Helen Keller

Beyond this Day

Because we are social creatures, we know that we are bound to other humans. We live in groups and usually do what we can to make the life of the group a little better for our having been a part of it. Our particular effect on those around us, like the values we pass down to our children, can be viewed as a kind of immortality. A sort of memory is in process. Life is continuing... beyond this hour, beyond this day. The title of our book, *Beyond This Day*, is simply an affirmation that we are not alone, that in the act of sharing or relating in a positive way we give keepsakes to those we love.

It is not only by our actions that we make a difference in people's lives, but also by our presence. We share who we are with others. And over time, we will have either a positive or a negative effect on them. We will either genuinely care for others or succumb to self-centeredness. We determine this. We will influence, to some degree, the emotional experiences of those close to us, experiences that will naturally continue in their memories long after we are gone.

And so it is with those who have passed before us. Quite often it is a fondness and deep regard for one close to us, cultivated over the course of the relationship that we remember and put to good use in our lives long after that loved one is no longer here. Even where there might have been discord, we can usually find a kernel of positive influence that flowed to us from the relationship. So we come to realize that certain profound influences upon us actually exist outside of time. They exist beyond the present, and the love engendered by them most certainly exists... beyond this day.

- 10 -

A Tribute

In this section you are invited to remember your loved one in some very special ways. A record of the funeral service itself is provided for those who, in years to come, will see how, when and where you bade your loved one farewell. A place for a photograph of the deceased will, of course, become one of the family treasures you pass on and a Family Register will be a handy record of a spouse and of children and grandchildren. Places are also provided to list friends who were near and dear to you in a difficult time as well as a place to remember your loved one's relationship to the community and the things your loved one stood for in life. Special times with your loved are precious memories. Your recollections in the *Times to Remember* section may someday provide for family members an inspirational keepsake unlike any other. Adding a reminiscence of your family life to this very personal documentation is a befitting testimonial to one you have loved and will remember always.

"To live in hearts we leave behind is not to die."

- Thomas Campbell

FUNERAL SERVICES
— for —

_____
Name of Deceased

SERVICES

_____
Location

_____
Officiating

_____
Date

BURIAL

_____
Cemetery Name

_____
Date of Interment   Section   Lot

INURNMENT

_____

A Tribute

Place Keepsake Photograph Here

Life in Community

A wider circle of friends.

Our lives are inextricably bound to our families, but we are also part of a wider circle of people. Some of this circle may share our most ardent beliefs as expressed through membership in a faith community; some may be dear friends from days gone by; and some we may know through civic or fraternal fellowship, bound together in a love for the community. The wider circle of our loved one may have included fellow military veterans, civic club associates, work colleagues, hobbyists and sports enthusiasts or other fellow travelers on a similar path. In our grief we take time to consider those who populated the wider circle of our loved one. We are grateful for them and we know they are grieving, too. For those departed, we keep their memory alive right along with that of our own loved one. Here we list our loved one's special interests and involvements in the community, along with those special friends that made up an ever widening circle.

Special friends in the community... Civic and fraternal memberships... Hobbies and interests...

What Our Loved One Stood For

*"Two roads diverged in a wood, and I –
I took the one less travelled by."
- Robert Frost*

    We all have guiding principles, stated or unstated, that help see us over the rough places and around the blind corners of life. For our loved one, these principles may have been expressed in the form of religious tenets or culled directly from personal experience; they may have been lessons hard won or passed down through generations of family values. Our loved one may have been energetically outspoken or quietly obedient to a set of life standards. Here we take time to briefly revisit those core beliefs that bolstered our loved one in life and that may even help us to cope with the great sorrow now upon us.

Memorable values of a life well-lived ...

The Stream of Time

"Time is but the stream I go a fishing in."

In Henry David Thoreau's brief quote above he described well the act of remembering. How wonderful the gift of memory can be when sweet recollections help heal our aching hearts. How therapeutic it can be to cast a line of memory into the stream of time and pull up hallowed moments. The remarkable endeavors, the prominent desires, the cherished dreams, fulfilled or not, are all the ingredients of an individual's life worth speaking of, worth citing for those left behind.

We might journey back to our first meeting with our loved one. Our reminiscence may contain the foreshadowing of a future together; perhaps we recall the carefree humor or things said early on that may have provided a foundation for deep feelings to come. There is usually in the record of a first meeting between couples, or between parent and newborn child or among closest friends, some semblance of affection flowing from one heart to another, some initial longing for togetherness that is well worth retrieving from the recesses of the mind. We have provided here a place for more of that journey back to a former time: a survey of a year or a snapshot of a moment, a description of a memorable event or a few written words as witness to a blessed history.

It is ours for the writing, our stream in which to drop a line ... anytime we're ready.

Times to Remember

"But be, as you have been, my happiness..."
- Randall Jarrell

Cherished memories ...

Times to Remember

Times to Remember

OUR FAMILY TREE

A Record of Our Uniqueness and the Continuity of Life

It has been a long standing tradition in families to keep track of ancestors and descendents by making a record of them in a family keepsake. Most families have one or more people who delve into the genealogical records. These folks are not only archivists with their collections of family photographs and memorabilia but they are also usually a well of family stories. Personal family keepsakes make genealogists of us all, for a treasured keepsake is a record of the heart, tracking over time the unique character that makes our families special.

In the following space we can trace our roots in a way that might someday be handed down to an interested family member. Family histories can serve to remind us of the continuity of life and therefore how blessed we are. We may find strength in our family tree, for it can serve as a chronicle of love to help us live through the sorrow that is now very much a part of that love.

Family Register

MARRIAGE

_____
Date   Location

SPOUSE

_____
Name

_____
Date of Birth   Birthplace

_____
Died   Where

SPOUSE

_____
Name

_____
Date of Birth   Birthplace

_____
Died   Where

Children & Grandchildren

_____ | _____
Name   *Spouse*

_____   _____
Child's Name   *Child's Name*

_____   _____
Child's Name   *Child's Name*

_____   _____
Child's Name   *Child's Name*

_____ | _____
Name   *Spouse*

_____   _____
Child's Name   *Child's Name*

_____   _____
Child's Name   *Child's Name*

_____   _____
Child's Name   *Child's Name*

_____ | _____
Name   *Spouse*

_____   _____
Child's Name   *Child's Name*

_____   _____
Child's Name   *Child's Name*

_____   _____
Child's Name   *Child's Name*

Children & Grandchildren

Name | *Spouse*

Child's Name | *Child's Name*

Child's Name | *Child's Name*

Child's Name | *Child's Name*

Name | *Spouse*

Child's Name | *Child's Name*

Child's Name | *Child's Name*

Child's Name | *Child's Name*

Name | *Spouse*

Child's Name | *Child's Name*

Child's Name | *Child's Name*

Child's Name | *Child's Name*

Reflections on Our Family

"Family life is the source of the greatest human happiness."
- Robert Havighurst

The happiness that grew from within the family points to a reality greater than any individual could experience in solitude. There are scenes that remain in the heart and in the mind for a lifetime.

Memories of home and family life... Remembering what made our family unique...

_____
_____
_____
_____
_____
_____
_____
_____
_____
_____

Family Photograph

Place Keepsake Photograph Here

Additional Family Members

"In the family, happiness is in the ratio in which each is serving the others, seeking one another's good, and bearing one another's burdens."
- Henry Ward Beecher

The consolation of other family members can at times be of great value to us. Whether the condolences come from one close, a cousin we grew up with, an aunt or uncle, a grandparent, or even a relative we don't know all that well, we are still family and we gathered in physical presence or in spirit to bid our loved one farewell. We treasure our kin relationships and remember them with fondness and affection. We list here those special extended family members with whom we have shared other relatives in common, and with whom we have shared our experience and our love.

_____   _____

_____   _____

_____   _____

_____   _____

_____   _____

_____   _____

_____   _____

_____   _____

_____   _____

Friends

Some friends are just always there for us.

What would we do without them? They have given us such comfort with their presence, their humor, their forbearance. They have made the good times better and the bad times more bearable. We are close because of their honesty and their caring. They have risked ill feeling by cracking through our walls and really getting to know us. In truth, they have loved us, even when we weren't completely lovable!

How can we show our appreciation? What can we do to pay them back? No recompense is ever adequate, of course, for true friendship is invaluable. We may thank them by our resolve to live on in spite of our sorrow and deep pain.

We list those friends here, those who brought food or spent time with us, those whose notes, even from out of town, touched us in special ways. We list the friends for whom we know we can count on for comfort and for consolation, the ones who have been and will continue to be with us for life, for death and for all the in-betweens.

_____   _____

_____   _____

_____   _____

_____   _____

_____   _____

_____   _____

PART TWO
A Time to Mourn

"We are put on earth a little space that we
may learn to bear the beams of love."
- William Blake

The Common Ground of our Grief

*"The heart has its reasons,
which reason does not know."*
—Blaise Pascal

Reasons of the Heart

A well known philosopher once said, "Life is not a problem to be solved but a mystery to be lived." And so it is with our grieving. We live the mystery of it, for our only balm is life itself. We learn to trust the heart's own reasons and that same heart is bound to take us places we certainly didn't expect to go.

Some try to make perfect sense of every emotion, pang of heartache and desperate question that arises from our loss. But grief is an individual experience that won't fit neatly into a box. No "system" of bereavement represents the be all and end all of research concerning matters of grief or loss. For one grieving, analysis always falls short. Perhaps the best we can do is speculate as to the common ground we may share when we suffer. There are no experts, no hard and fast formulas. There is only the experience that you are going through at this moment. We cannot tell you what you should be feeling or how you should be reacting. But perhaps, to a small degree, through this keepsake volume, we might be able to be present with you as you walk this lonesome road.

Of course we do see some things similar in the emotional struggles of those in mourning. There are indeed common denominators of our sorrow, the undeniable "reasons of the heart." There are also special issues in our grief, in the "mystery to be lived", that many of us will struggle to address. These common feelings and special issues do not represent any kind of time line of our grief or any kind of inevitable emotions we should or should not be experiencing. Whatever you may be feeling, it is our sincere desire that you may find here a glimpse of the hope and the strength that reside in the recesses of your heart.

The Shock of What Has Happened

News of the death of a loved one, even if expected, is always a surprise. It is hard for our hearts and minds to grasp. And often we find ourselves asking a most profound question: "What has just happened?" For answers, we rely upon the wisdom of the ages, upon our own particular religious tenets, if appropriate, or upon information about death available to us from a variety of sources. But the question is not a question of the mind; it is a question of the heart. And our hearts feel the shock of great loss. We may come to understand that the heart really does have its reasons, which reason doesn't know. And the heart also has questions that cannot be answered with words. A kind of sad bewilderment can come over us. But our wondering doesn't so much call out for an answer as it does some kind of expression of love. Only love, the love we felt (and still feel) for the deceased, the love they shared with us, the love we have encountered from others in the midst of our sorrow and the love we have given to others hurting from their own loss, can inform our hearts when the question arises. We know in a profound sense that something has ended and something has begun. And we know that, somehow, love is at the center of it all.

Emotional Avoidance

For some of us the actual fact of our loss is too much to take in all at once. We might almost unconsciously seek ways to keep from thinking about it.

Emotional avoidance is a natural phenomenon, and so we might hear ourselves saying, "I know Mom is gone, but I just can't believe it; I can't believe that if I went to her house right now she wouldn't be sitting at her kitchen table reading as she always did." Losing someone so dear is literally unbelievable. Yet if emotional avoidance is natural, so is human resiliency, and, in time, we may begin to look as straightforward at our new life as our heart will allow us. It is important to note that, though the intensity of our grief does wane, it is not necessarily something that begins and ends in a conventional time frame. Though we accommodate our loss with new and creative strategies for continuing life, still our loss is something that lives in us and becomes a part of what makes us who we are. The sadness at a loved one's death helps to define us, just as does the great and abiding strength of our love.

Facing The Pain

The pain of our loss can be devastating. There can be an indescribable emptiness that is implanted in us. The pain is so tangible it may even manifest itself in medical symptoms such as high blood pressure, depression, a decrease in appetite or binge eating, digestive problems, headaches or any other of a number of physical signs. People with pre-existing conditions such as diabetes, heart disease, allergies or any other disorders need to be especially cognizant of the fact that their symptoms may surge during this difficult time.

Sometimes we are helped by friends and family and sometimes their well-meaning acts of kindness seem nothing more than imposing and intrusive. A grieving heart, like a wounded animal, escapes the clearing and seeks sanctuary. It longs for a suitable refuge where it will find its own healing powers. We know that hiding from the pain in alcohol abuse or the abuse of medication only prolongs the suffering and takes our despondency to another level. So we live with and in the pain. And sometimes we don't know our way out of it. But all along this solemn path, flickers of light have begun to catch our attention: someone's presence, a consoling word or gesture, aid from a surprising source. We ignore them until we cannot any longer. And then we begin to respond from the heart. We manage a few steps. We struggle to rise up and make our way, forever changed, to the clearing once again. And invariably as we are making it to that clearing, the people we love are standing there.

THE SEARCH

As we suffer the loss of a loved one we may begin to search our minds and hearts. *What could I have done better? Could I have been a better son or daughter, mother or father?* We may start the mental "what-ifs". *What if I had paid them more attention? What if we could have reconciled more of the past?* The list goes on. Relationships have so many emotional tributaries that self blame is usually found floating down one of them. It is as natural as grief itself and self-reflection is part of the search. A death in the family may bring up old wounds or new doubts, dyed-in-the-wool beliefs or never-before-experienced speculation. It may call to mind our most mundane moments or our most profound. We search for answers about ways to continue living. We search the hidden places of our hearts; we reflect upon life itself, a natural part of which is the death that has just entered it.

When Grief Lingers

Grief is an individual experience that we live through in our own way. Most of us eventually learn to live with our loss and the deeply felt connections to our loved one. And yet, for some, the pain lingers on and can even become debilitating for the one suffering through it.

Some term this Prolonged Grief Disorder (PGD) or "Complicated Grief". However we term it, we know that a percentage of people experience their grief in this way. Those living through this type of grief are not "indulgent" or unwilling to call on their inner strengths; they want to be able to live with loss as much as anyone and, with help, they can and will. Symptoms of Complicated Grief may include: inattentiveness, bitterness, psychological numbness, identity confusion and lack of trust in others, and an overall inability to make life adjustments to the death of the loved one. Sometimes even day to day functional impairment may be experienced and depression may begin to play a large role in one's life.

If possible, one experiencing these symptoms may want to seek treatment specifically related to the particular characteristics that mark the disorder. This is a time when caring friends and family should abstain from judgment and encourage help, perhaps from clinician experienced with Complicated Grief. This a real disorder and, when treated, can open the door to recovery and a new sense of freedom and desire for life. Others in the helping fields are learning more about Complicated Grief and are certainly willing to be of help. And just as all grief is individual, so too is all healing. One of the glories of the human spirit is that it is always seeking to revitalize itself so that even in the face of suffering or lingering sorrow, hope may reign.

The Invitation

The word "Invitation" comes from the Latin *en vitare*, that is, "into life". We do many things with invitations. Some we receive and then stick in a drawer to think about later. Some we attach to the refrigerator to help us remember to respond. Some we can't decide if we want to accept or not, so we procrastinate in our response. And so it is with our return to daily life and the ordinary things that make it up. The malaise of sorrow keeps tugging at us and the thought of going about our daily routine is either most welcome or a dreaded thing. The phrase "life goes on" can either be a great relief or an insult to the painful process we are experiencing. Still, the invitation is out there. We may put it out of sight and out of mind; we may keep pondering it, finding ourselves unable to respond; we may linger in the throes of indecision. Or we may understand that we are already accepting an invitation by our willingness to experience our grief. It is all in our own time and at our own pace, and we determine the manner in which we accept the invitation, the way we continue "into life."

SPECIAL ISSUES OF OUR GRIEF
The Fear

Some great fears associated with our loss may appear in the form of questions: *What am I going to do now? How will I live? What is going to be different and how can I be alone after all these years? How will others in the family fare?* We may fear the family dynamic will change in such a way that members will drift apart. There is also the strange fear of the unknown, of impending doom; the sense that the sky might just fall after all, for we are no longer complete.

Some say the antidote to fear is knowledge, but knowledge sometimes, as Shakespeare said, "...maketh a bloody entrance." Some lessons are hard lessons. And knowledge alone cannot do the job. Trust accompanied by knowledge is a much better defense against the stinging fear that can grip us. We use our hard won knowledge of living with grief, and we add the trust that experience tells us will see us through. We trust that life will go on, that the love that was shared with the deceased will still bear fruit in times to come, that parts of the relationship with our loved one actually do continue and stay with us even as we walk through the fear.

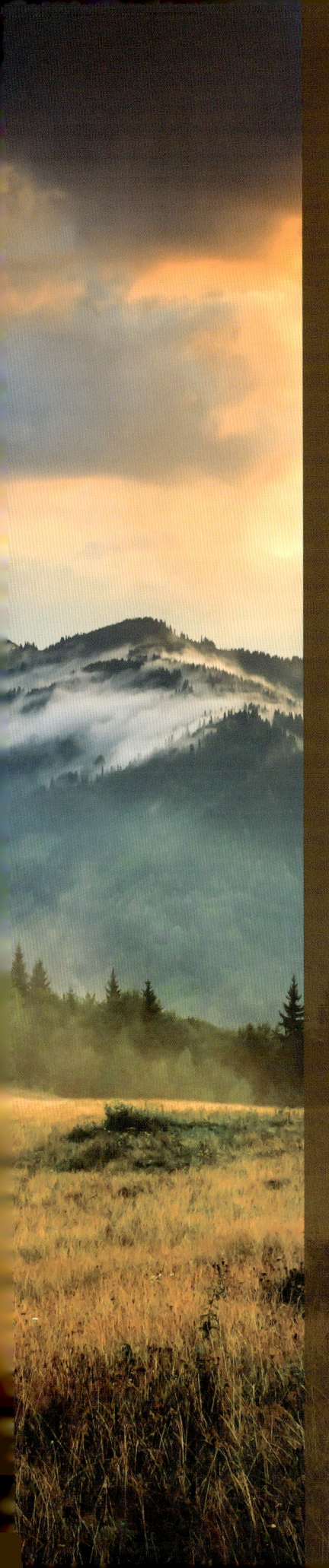

SPECIAL ISSUES OF OUR GRIEF
The Sorrow

Self-pity is an emotion sometimes ridiculed as indulgent and selfish. But sometimes we simply feel sorry for ourselves in the same way we might feel sorry for someone else. This kind of sorrow may not be the demon some make it out to be; only when we become frozen in it is it counter productive to our healing. At times we tend to get too clinical about our powerfully felt emotions, as if there is only one way to handle them. We lick our wounds in different ways. So be it. Our culture will find a thousand ways to try to deny the incisive wound of death. We do it with alcohol and other drugs just as we do it with psychological models that make our agony somehow unacceptable. Something bad has happened; it hurts; we feel sorry for the world who never knew our loved one and we feel sorry for ourselves because we will miss our loved one and cherish their memory long after any vestige of self-pity has vanished.

SPECIAL ISSUES OF OUR GRIEF
The Guilt

Guilt is another much maligned emotion in modern times. Some guilt can move us to improve our actions and correct ourselves when we are on an erroneous path. If we have neglected someone then we will feel this negative emotion and it may help us become more attentive to those we love. But we need not place an unjust burden on our own shoulders. We all let each other down at times and many of us focus on those times while ignoring the particular joys we may have wrought or the genuine charity for which we may have been responsible. True humility moves us to accept our shortcomings and try to amend them as well as to recognize our good qualities and cultivate them. Guilt can also turn to shame, that is, the guilt for just being. After a death we may even feel guilty for being alive, but time usually helps us understand that, although we may never fully grasp the whys and wherefores of our loved one's passing, still we have a place in the world and we carry with us a little bit of our loved one wherever we go.

SPECIAL ISSUES OF OUR GRIEF
The Sense of Betrayal

Though we don't say it, in our loneliness we may feel as if our loved has somehow betrayed us. We may feel betrayed simply because we are now alone. We yearn to have had more time. There may be a hundred variations of circumstance that contribute to our feeling betrayed by the person who has died or even by life itself.

On the other hand we may feel that we betrayed our loved one and we sink into an abyss of shame for having let them down. Perhaps we just weren't there; or devoted enough or the caretaker we wanted to be or should have been. Betrayal is a lingering, odious kind of quality that stings deeply and can ravage our hearts.

Not all that we grapple with is always good for us. Some twistings of the mind and heart can best be left to mystery and be done with. Death can be a temptress, calling out our worst fears and shining light on the traits we most abhor, in ourselves or in our loved ones. This is when we find the goodness that exists in every relationship and we bring our spirit to bear upon it. We pay homage to that goodness. We trust that somewhere in the realm of that goodness there is mercy and understanding and we give ourselves over to it. Slowly and surely, day by day, the sense of betrayal is left to the wind and, in our deepest thoughts and simplest acts, we give ourselves over to goodness.

SPECIAL ISSUES OF OUR GRIEF
The Memories

    Our memories tell the story of our lives, a winding story with many plotlines and settings, major characters and minor, heroes and villains. Our departed loved ones wrote their life stories by what they believed in and what they did, by who they loved and who they became. Our memories come and go, allowing nature to reveal to us what it will. The bad times can sometimes bleed into the narrative and we get stuck with them. It may even be necessary to consciously recall the good times to come to the rescue, and they will. The lives of others have been imprinted onto our own. They live in us and the memory of them is a kind of immortality that teaches us to continue making our own memories, for we too live in others that love us.

    We may fear we will begin to forget our loved one. Accompanying this feeling can be a sense that we are abandoning them. We want to keep them in our mind's eye, a portrait enshrined in our heart. In a poem about the act of remembering, William Butler Yeats compared it to mountain grasses that keep the form of the animal that laid there once. The gradual release of the image is Nature's way, yet memory holds on in fidelity:

> *Because the mountain grass*
> *Cannot but keep the form*
> *Where the mountain hare has lain.*

    Something of our deceased loved one will always be with us, even if not perfectly retained in the senses. We can rest assured that somewhere, perhaps even in the way we have come to see things or react to the world, our loved one still exists, still eloquently outlined in the grass, still warmly imprinted upon our hearts.

SPECIAL ISSUES OF OUR GRIEF
The Unresolved

Loving bonds are always tested and living by the Golden Rule is not always easy. At any given moment in our history with others there are bound to be issues of the heart left unresolved. It is the nature of love to strive to make whole what is not whole. And it is in this striving that we find ourselves. It is in this striving that we learn the importance of other people in our lives. Human relationships are never absolutely whole or perfect, the failings among us all, the small poverties of spirit can serve, even with the death of our loved ones, to bring us closer. To love is to fall short of perfection but to retain hope in our hearts and mend what fences we can along the way. We come to understand that love doesn't need resolution so much as promise. And the promise of our love, even for one who is gone, is still being kept.

The Loneliness

The quiet, but desperate pain of loneliness might be the greatest cross we bear. It's like a part of our own being is missing. The blessing and the curse is that we still feel the presence of our departed loved one. It darts about our mind and spirit with astounding poignancy. That felt presence can be a unique balm in the toughest days of our grief. And even though others are not the quick fix, still the presence of friends and family can be of great comfort. Perhaps our biggest job in life is to be present for others and to connect with that presence. In so doing we touch the cause of our deepest pain and the herald of our truest joy.

SPECIAL ISSUES OF OUR GRIEF
The Despair

We seldom talk about the hopeless state of being we refer to as despair. It almost falls into that region of taboo topics, as if it were somehow inhuman to feel utterly despondent and confused. Yet it is a most human feeling that has been visited upon some of the strongest, most spiritual among us. And grieving the loss of a loved one can certainly call it to the fore. The beginnings of despair can lead us to face some of the greatest issues of all: the will to live, the path to faith and trust, the notion of purpose in one's life. Obviously, if we didn't believe strongly that life is worth living, that everyone's journey has purpose, this volume wouldn't exist. Experience teaches us that as we gradually become transformed by our sorrows and our suffering, that as we rise above our deep pain, we demonstrate to others the human dignity that is a part of our essence. Victor Frankl, in his powerful story of life in a German concentration camp, spoke of working in the frozen fields early mornings and waiting for a distant farmhouse light to come on, for that light became his great symbol of faith and endurance. A simple farmhouse light became a remarkable sign of the existence of something greater than evil and pain and brokenness. He drew from that particular light and the layers of meaning light itself brought to him, a strength that became a great example of the resiliency and generosity of the human spirit. So, too, in our own quiet way, do we call forth the light we know lives in us. In the beams of this light, in the love that we continue to share with those around us, despair has little chance.

Hope and Gratitude... A Day at a Time

The simple cliché, *One Day at a Time* has actually been a life saver for many people. The brief maxim is so popular because it is a prescription for confronting any number of the various realities of human life, be it addiction, disappointment, physical hardship, painful loss or any other dire set of circumstances we may encounter. In our grief we sometimes find ourselves taking the situation a day, an hour, even a minute at a time. The ability to live with this perspective is wired into us, for if it was not we would constantly project our lives into the future or stay buried in the past, rendering us completely unable to react to the immediate challenges of day to day life. Indeed, we find, we are able to make it through this given day. And if we can make it through today, there is hope for tomorrow.

The day-at-a-time perspective does not mean we don't cherish the past or even bring forth from it therapeutic strategies to help us in our grieving. Indeed, being able to live in the present often fosters a special gratitude for the blessings of the past. We are grateful for the relationship that once was, grateful for all we learned from our loved one, grateful we became a part of each other. It also doesn't mean that we can never make future plans or envision our lives in the fragile weeks ahead. It simply means that we don't project ourselves into the future in some evasive daydream to keep us from walking through our pain. We are given hope by living in the present. We try to live today, taking from our difficulties as well as the little streams of relief that will seep in as days become more days, the gifts our loved one would want us to receive, the gifts of endurance and acceptance, the gifts of hope and gratitude, of life lived as fully as possible, a day at a time.

All Grief is Special

Every death is the death of an individual and every grief is as individual as the one left behind trying to live through it. Each grieving person brings their particular belief system, their personal experience and their own personality to bear on the matters at hand. But these are not the only variables in the grieving process. Who passed away and the way they passed is also determinate of how we grieve.

Experiencing the sorrow that accompanies the death of a loved one is always difficult. But because each type of relationship with each different loved one is different, we may feel very different feelings as we mourn. The following section takes a look at how our grief may be altered by who it is that has died and how they died. It is not inclusive of every situation but is meant rather to empathize with each individual grieving, no matter how their loved one died or whether they have lost a spouse, parent, child, sibling, grandparent, special relative or close friend.

Just as we bring our own individuality to the place of sorrow, we also bring that individuality to the "living through" process, the same individual strength that has seen us through many other trials. In this section it is our hope to tap into that personal strength as we reflect on many of the personal experiences of grief.

ALL GRIEF IS SPECIAL

LOVE NEVER FAILS...
On the death of a spouse

Widows know the pain of losing a part of oneself; the loneliness as real as their own "one" flesh. From the tragic death of a young spouse to the merciful demise of a long time mate who has suffered with declining health or the toll of years, the one left behind feels their heart breaking. And yet, in the hidden recesses of the heart, they yearn for consolation and hope.

There is no greater sacrifice than saying goodbye, than living through the heavy days and lonesome nights; no courage greater than that of a widowed spouse resisting the temptation to withdraw from life. To simply pick up the phone or answer the door can take heroic effort. Living through the grief becomes a conscious endeavor that takes patience and strength. Acceptance of a spouse's death and a subsequent new way of living does not just happen. It is crafted in forbearance, trust and the invaluable help of those who care.

Many widows have found help from support groups specializing in the unique manifestations of their grief. Many of those widowed have eventually found strength in being of service to others, especially those going through what they have endured. At some point we learn that we can live even with a heart torn asunder. Just as we were forever changed by our beloved spouse so can we live the lessons of that great bond and by so doing let others know that not only does love never fail... it also never ends.

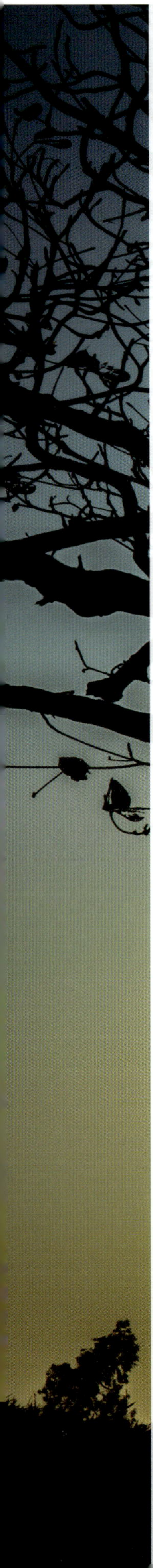

All Grief is Special

The Long Bond of Love...
On the death of a parent

The grief surrounding the death of a parent comes with a history. Sometimes that history is a chronicle of fondness and emotional nourishment, of lessons well-learned and decades of discovery. Sometimes, however, it is a history spotted with difficulty, shadowed by emotional distances or the unfinished business of the heart. Perhaps we lived far away and had too little contact with our parents or perhaps we were dutiful caregivers weakened by the rigors of that unsung job. We may find ourselves struggling with guilt or forgiveness or both. We confront an emptiness of spirit that longs for comfort. Regardless of the particulars, we are significantly changed by the death of a parent. And our perspective is challenged by a well of bittersweet memory.

There may be hard times ahead, especially if a living parent is struggling with being alone. There may be burdensome fiduciary responsibilities or practical family issues that collide with the grieving process. We may also be surprised by a grief that comes upon us sometime long after the funeral, when we least expect to find a sea of emotion rising up from the depths. Relationships as powerful as these do not end; they merely change. And in the changing they become more uniquely our own. We memorialize our parents with family stories told to our own children or in the discovery of our siblings in a new light. We face the reality of guilt through soul searching honesty, heartfelt reflection and in the wisdom of others with whom we may trust our saddened heart. We open ourselves to forgiving and being forgiven. It is a time for gentleness and healing. And the hearts and hands of those who love us are ever near and ready.

OUR VERY OWN...
On the death of a child

What loss is greater than a child's death? We feel "diminished" as never before, for a child's life is meant to unfold in growth and maturity, a testament to the marvelous handiwork of nature. So how can it be that our child is gone? Some blame themselves or even life itself. But the efforts of finite minds fall short of understanding. The hurt is almost unbearable.

We trudge through our sorrow in slow motion, moment by moment. The rituals enacted for other deaths in the family: graveside visits or stories about the deceased, are painful but no less necessary to the grieving process. Some families have found solace in the establishment of memorials that pertain to the lives of young people, such as special school initiatives or funds for childhood diseases. Gestures of this kind are anything but empty. They can resonate in positive ways for years to come.

Love slowly embraces us and walks with us on the long and difficult road ahead. We may find ourselves avoiding children to keep from breaking down. Our sorrow may be unimaginably intense. But we must hear with our hearts in this distressed time, for there are others who have experienced something akin to our pain and we may need to seek their counsel and companionship. There is a growing awareness of the efficacy of support groups for those who have lost a child. In time, because a child's giving spirit was woven in with ours, we are able to help someone else whose sorrow is overwhelming. And in that moment of charity our child has truly come to life in a new and unique way.

All Grief is Special

Our Flesh and Blood...
On the death of a sibling

When a sibling passes away we sometimes find ourselves returning emotionally to the days of childhood. We may feel a sense of unfairness when a younger sibling dies. And with one older we may have a sense of loss similar to the losing of a parent. This wound can affect the whole system of family relationships in sometimes confusing ways. One sibling may have been the peacemaker in the family, another the main caretaker in regard to parents. A death among siblings can shake the foundation of these established roles. Some siblings have stayed closer over the years than others and these brothers or sisters may now have to look to others for support and comfort.

Often weakened family ties have been refashioned due to the shared grief over a sibling's death. In honor of the deceased, new and helpful family alliances may form that actually give strength to individual family members. But it should not be surprising or considered in any way disloyal to feel the need for counsel from outside the family. Great gifts can come from those we least expect. Nor should we be surprised if "childlike" feelings re-emerge as we grieve our brother or sister's passing. The child inside of us demands attention but it is the adult we have become who tends to those feelings, therefore we do so with care and with a respect for what once existed in the life of our family. And in this way, we truly honor the memory of dear brother or sister who has gone on.

Our Living History...
On the death of a grandparent

The death of a grandparent brings added dimensions of sorrow to our grief. Aside from the closeness that recalls special experiences of our youth, our sorrow also responds to our culture's view of the elderly. The last years, months or weeks of an older person's life can present puzzling and sometimes complex medical decisions for families. There is a greater likelihood of an impersonal atmosphere surrounding the death of a loved one. These difficult situations can certainly affect the way in which we grieve. Even in the best of circumstances when a grandparent passes away an era ends. A precious part of our living family history is gone. The wisdom imparted, the stories told, the way they made us laugh and the questions only they had the answers to are all now stilled. In the quiet we reflect upon this cherished person and upon their place in our family's life. These reflections are natural to the grieving process and they can lead us to a greater recognition of our own humanity. Perhaps we look differently at older people we encounter. We understand a little more about our own aging. And we greatly appreciate the continuing influence our grandparent still has on us to this very day.

All Grief is Special

A Captive Heart...
On the death of a special relative

We have all had those special relatives who captured our hearts over the years: an uncle who had a knack for entertaining kids, an aunt whose cookies and stories we will never forget or a cousin who was more like a sister or brother. There was just something special about our relationship that we both knew and felt: a kindred spirit, a way of seeing things. We may have shared much and, in that sharing, formed an unassailable bond.

The void left when we lose a special relative like this is always difficult to endure. Few may understand how deep the connection was. So where do we go for comfort? With whom may we now speak of this special friendship? Perhaps only those who have had the same kind of relationship with a special relative know the weight of our sorrow. Only they know how endearing a familial friendship can be. Sometimes we feel these relationships are few and far between, but perhaps there are more of them out there than we may have thought at first.

However we find comfort, a part of it will be in having a place in our hearts for these special relatives, and no coping mechanism will take that away. We now reflect more intimately on those others who have lost special relatives and we understand together that certain relatives will always live inside of us, their spirit helping animate us along our way, their memory forever cherished.

Like the Shelter of a Tree...
On the death of a close friend

Experiences shared over the course of time, similar ideals and values as well as a kind of indescribable compatibility are all qualities characteristic of close friendships. Somewhere along the line we found a person who would be there for us when support or comfort or help of some kind was needed, like the shelter of a tree in the summer sun or when sudden showers fall. Close friends give of themselves because generosity is part of the defining characteristic of the relationship.

These friendships make for hard good-byes. This friend may have been a special link to childhood memories or a surprise companion of our later years. The friendship may have been there for decades or have just begun its development. It was sustained in love, however, and it is that shared love that makes their passing so hard to take.

Where do we go to be consoled? After all, it was so often this very friend who consoled us in difficult times. We go of course to our own hearts and our memories keep the friendship alive.

We may never find as good a friend but this friendship has taught us something about the nature of love itself. Perhaps we become a beacon for the lonely, for we know that unending love appeared in a person to whom we became very close. And we know that kind of love never ends, but is passed on... friend to friend.

THE GRIEF OF A CHILD

Because children are so naturally resilient, we may not fully comprehend the depth of their grief. Like adults, they experience grief in a highly individual manner, but there are common responses to a loved one's death more typical of children that deserve close attention.

Because children are so tactile in their daily lives, emotional stress or confusion often exhibits itself physically as in a lack of appetite or digestive problems. Treating the physical symptoms is only part of our concern. Taking time for the common sense, loving answers to questions that will naturally arise is a labor of love well worth our efforts. We might also address this tactile element of their being by letting the children handle personal items of the deceased: Grandpa's sweater, a sibling's toy, a parent's personal belonging that may become a cherished keepsake.

Grieving children may also have nightmares, exhibit overtly aggressive behavior at school or play or even regress to behaviors typically associated with a younger age. Their paramount need is for our time and our presence. Making things as simple as possible for children by providing daily structure may also help. We let them know that it is O.K. to have feelings of anger and frustration. It is also common for children to blame themselves for the death in the family. We might consult a professional counselor who can help us navigate these delicate waters. We also let them see us begin the essential process of memorializing our departed loved one. It may or may not be appropriate for children to attend the funeral, depending upon their age and maturity level, but honoring our loved one in stories, prayers, scrapbooks and other memorials can be a moving and instructive way to begin the healing process.

Finally, as we tend to our precious children in their grief, we become acutely aware of their ability to live in the present and their knack for finding joy. Yes, we are there to care for the children in their fear and their sorrow but they are there for us, too, in their courage, resilience and vitality.

How We Lost Them

The manner in which a loved one has passed away has everything to do with the kind of grief we subsequently experience. The manifestations of grief we have already discussed represent commonly shared ways of coping with great loss, but the particular context of that loss also affects us in highly individual ways. Here we briefly discuss the nature of our loss depending upon the circumstances surrounding the death of our loved one. Of course there is something uniquely personal in all experiences of grief and no two individuals react identically to loss. But however our loved one has passed, there are threads of empathy to be discovered by opening our hearts to others. However the death occurs, the common bond of those left behind is great and abiding love.

"Where there is great love, there are always miracles."

- Willa Cather

How We Lost Them

A Vigil Kept

Forbearance is a virtue that certainly comes into play when a protracted illness envelopes the life of a family. This can be a great challenge, especially for primary caregivers. These times can be almost unbearable, but caregivers stay the course and give what aid they can, learning the hard way that death can be the height of mercy and peace.

Sometimes long illnesses can be financially overwhelming for a family. These wounds can bring out the worst in us if we do not proceed cautiously. Many times a financial advisor can be of help when the medical or nursing care costs are growing. There are increasing numbers of professionals specializing in these areas today.

A long illness can also be physically and emotionally wearing upon family and friends. Having someone to talk with about what the family is going through may well be helpful. This may be a professional such as a psychologist or other counselor; it may be a member of the clergy trained to help with these kinds of problems or it may be a caring friend in whom we have great confidence.

One thing we found in this painful process was how to recognize the special moments when our loved one either consciously or unconsciously taught us great lessons. It may have been a special gesture to a child, a small utterance of wisdom, a forgiving nod or perhaps a glance that seemed to come from another world. If we have those moments, we cherish them; if not we still know that our vigil kept was good and right and giving, for the only viable response to suffering is love. And in that case, the special moment may just have been our own love freely given to another.

"The higher goal of spiritual living is not to amass a wealth of information, but to find sacred moments."

- Abraham Heschel

How We Lost Them

A Natural Course

Medical technology has not only made astounding progress in battling the effects of many once debilitating and fatal diseases, it has also extended our life spans considerably in the last fifty years. This wonderful progress, however, has at times created bewildering end-of-life issues. When once an elder may have died of what was called "natural causes" most likely in their own home, today we rely on the compassionate caregivers of institutions to fill some of the roles family once did and families are sometimes forced to make very difficult decisions with regard to the prolongation of a loved one's life. Though hospice organizations, along with very special caregivers in many hospital settings, are gallantly entering into the life of the family to offer aid, expertise and comfort, still, quite often the last days of our loved one are spent away from home in an institutional setting. This all too common set of circumstances makes it all the more important to bring to a loved one's passing a sense of human dignity, a realization that even the pain of living and of dying has redeeming qualities that live on in loved ones.

And when one we love has lived long and the natural course of events has escorted them to life's end, we look beyond the seemingly unnatural departure common to modern society and give thanks for a long life, perhaps one that allowed for the wisdom only years can bring. We might be grateful for the experience of grandchildren in our loved one's life or for other joys that are possible in the golden years.

And our gratitude for the life of an elder who has passed will be noticed by others, especially the younger members of the family. To plant with them the seed that says cherish life in all its forms is an invaluable gift to enjoy, even in the midst of sorrow and grief.

"...any man's death diminishes me, because I am involved in Mankind; And therefore never send to know for whom the bell tolls; It tolls for thee."

- John Donne

How We Lost Them

A Sudden Blow

Death is rarely welcomed, but many times expected. It may come as a result of a serious illness or the natural course of time. Families sometimes see warning signs, especially in the case of the older members. But sometimes death comes as a jolting surprise. Perhaps a young person in the prime of life is suddenly struck down or a tragedy of inestimable proportion wounds a family and its friends as deeply as one may be wounded. It may be from the devastation of war or a blind accident. We question it almost obsessively yet everything remains shrouded in mystery. Families and friends hold onto each other. With sudden tragedies we must put aside differences and bond together, using each other's strength as defense against the pain of such profound sorrow.

But even in the absence of such care we must find a way to cope. There may have been so much left unsaid, so many hurdles left yet in the relationship. Where do we take our residue of agony? We search our spiritual lives for the help we need and the results of that search direct us onward. We search our hearts for some manner of expressing the void left in our life.

There is no way around a broken heart. But with the broken heart is a sense of what others have felt before us and what others will feel when a sudden blow strikes at a loved one. We may be their only refuge, a true refuge because we understand this special wound. And someday we may hold another's hand as they walk through it.

"The hand of death is ever... too untimely and sudden..."

- Pliny the Younger

A Special Circumstance

Sometimes the death of a loved one carries the added weight of tragedy due to controversy, violence, despair or any number of other confounding circumstances. Our nation holds in its heart the particularly tragic remnants of Pearl Harbor and 9/11; the devastating tornadoes and powerful hurricanes of our history; the sick trails of serial killers and the abhorrent evil of senseless acts of terror. And as a people we carry that weight in our grief. The violence in our schoolyards, the utter heartbreak over a suicide, the devastation Nature sometimes unleashes, the tragedy of terminal disease, the pure sadness associated with any loss of a child, a military, law enforcement or first responder line of duty death, all of these special circumstances and more bring with them a burden beyond the grief itself.

With any of a number of special circumstances, we may become angry at society's insensitivity to the situation, at friends not understanding, at ourselves for what we perceive we might have been able to do and even at the deceased for leaving us in such a fashion. These forms of anger are common and may perhaps play a larger role in the grieving process when special circumstances are present. Special circumstances can also bring a sense of irrational guilt. We imagine some solution we could have engendered but did not, when reason tells us otherwise.

There is no "solution" to living with this type of grief. The human heart is embattled and we incur the wounds. Helpful professionals may come to our aid, for the maze of sad bewilderment can lead to great depression. We may draw near to people we trust. Support groups have been of great help to many in such difficult times. We know we must live this mystery, but we must also find a measure of peace and even joy that is a part of the human family. We must be gentle with ourselves; it is a time for great care.

"Only in the agony of parting do we look into the depths of love."

- George Eliot

How We Lost Them

A Distant Light

When one we care about is at death's door, we instinctively go to them. We offer our presence for them and for the rest of the family and friends. And yet, there are times when situations prevent our being there. Perhaps we live across the country and cannot get to the bedside in time; perhaps the death is as a result of a sudden tragedy and we are unable to be with family and friends for the funeral; perhaps special circumstances call for the need to refrain from being there. The distance, for whatever reason, seems unbearable. There is an inability to make it all real. We feel almost disembodied, separated from something essential. Indeed, not being present goes against our instincts and can even wreak havoc with us emotionally.

Where do we turn? How do we cope with the void? What do we do? We turn to friends, counselors, clergy or some other understanding persons who can empathize with us. What is pent up in us need not be kept inside, for we feel isolated enough as it is. We cope in part by memorializing this loved one we could not be with. We remember, perhaps through a journal or in other ways, our special connection. We might also talk to those who were present and share with them what we might have shared had we been able to attend. We break the distance down as much as we can through communication and long distance caring. We cherish the memory of our loved one, for love and memory have no physical bounds; they travel the world and are able to touch far away hearts. Even though a distance has made the mournful time even more so, still love shared is a distant light that may help someone lost find their way.

Sweet is the memory of distant friends! Like the mellow rays of the departing sun, it falls tenderly, yet sadly, on the heart.

-Washington Irving

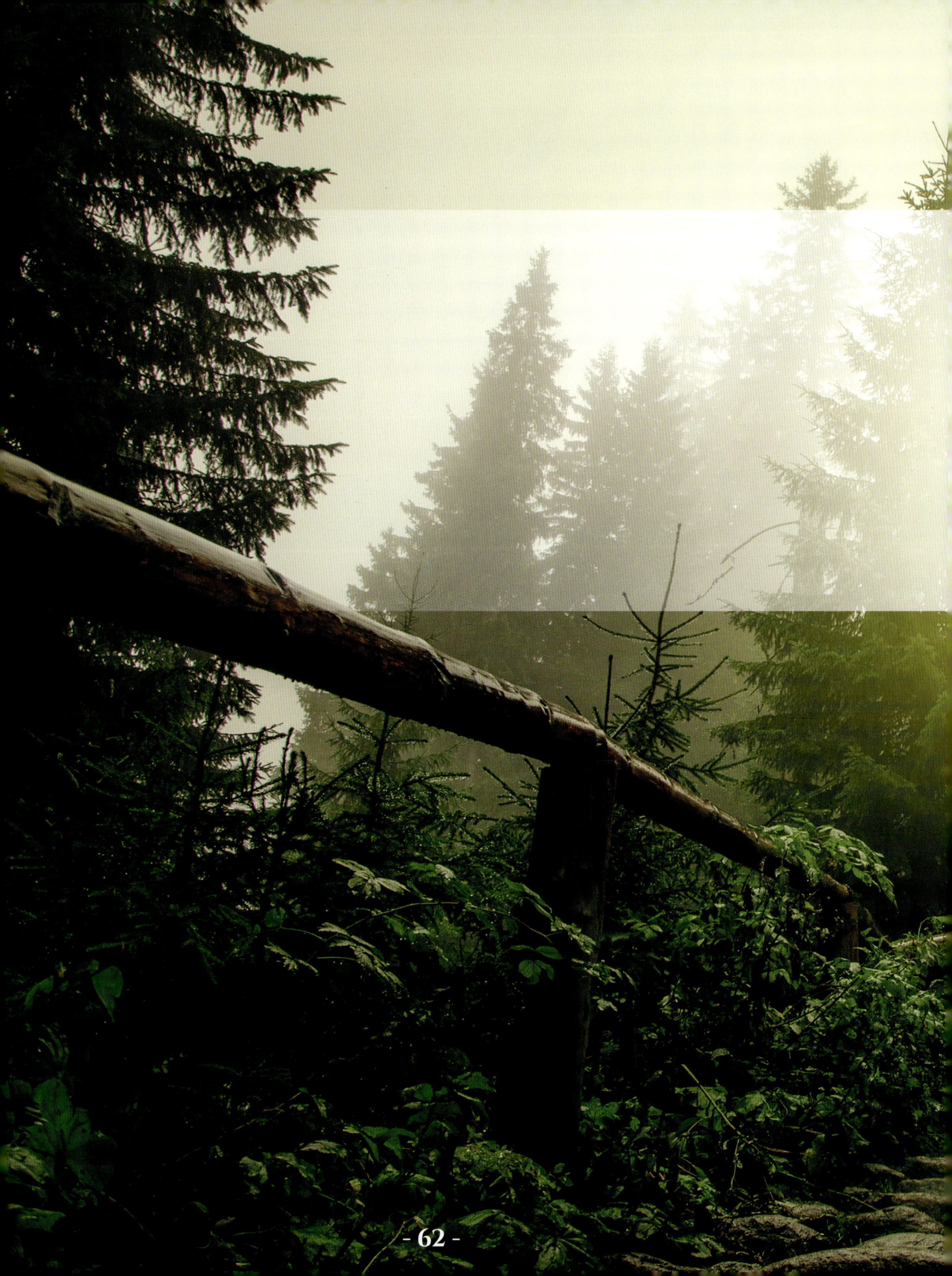

PART THREE
SEASONS OF FEELING

"The woods are lovely, dark and deep,
but I have promises to keep,
And miles to go before I sleep,
And miles to go before I sleep"
— Robert Frost

With Grace and Hope...
A Year of Aftercare

Each and every month something reminds us of our deceased loved ones. From the first frost to daffodils to the setting sun where sea meets shore, Mother Nature brings to mind in a thousand ways the dearest people with whom we have shared our love. Grief can sometimes become trapped inside our minds and our hearts, like a nestling in a hard rain. When the storm finally passes, however, things slowly come to life again and the birdsongs resume.

The first year is generally the hardest. The term "Aftercare" doesn't really describe what we are going through. Yes, it is after a funeral, after memorials, condolences and the gathering of family and friends. But it is not after a life, for that life still lives in us in as many ways as the sun rises and sets, in as many colors as the leaves turn, in as many kinds of wildflowers that dot wilderness paths and in as many blankets of snow that come down as we sleep.

With the passage of time we continue to affirm what we believe in, who we are and who we want to become as the seasons change and as we grow through our grief.

For each month we find a meditation as well as an affirmation. And with each month a beautiful illustration is offered to bring a sense of reflection and serenity to the text. Nature intends the passages of time to help us heal. But love is not bound by time. As we heal, we defy the calendar; we go beyond the season, the month, the week. We go with grace and hope...beyond this day.

"Our duty is to preserve what the past has had to say for itself, and to say for ourselves what shall be true for the future."

- John Ruskin

Seasons of Feeling

MONTHLY MEDITATIONS
ONE THING AT A TIME

Someone once defined meditation simply as *doing one thing at a time*. Doing *one thing* requires a concentrated, but relaxed focus on what lay before us. Meditating does not necessarily mean assuming a certain posture or chanting a mantra. It does presuppose, however, a willingness to slow down, to breathe deeply and let our thoughts venture in a certain direction, without succumbing to the many items on our daily "to do" lists. To be willing to experience the healing powers of meditation is to allow a few soothing words or images to help us focus, to help us do *one thing*. That one thing may be reading or listening to music or sitting quietly in a favorite chair, letting our thoughts ebb and flow like sea to shore. Meditation need not be silent and sedate but it is a giving over to the healing power residing in our own hearts and minds. Our *one thing* may be a walk in the sunshine, putting together a scrapbook of revered old photos, talking to a friend or playing catch with a son or daughter. It may be a reading or a simple affirmation as offered here for each month of the year. Our sorrow invites us to take time. We try taking a few minutes on a regular basis to relax and focus. We find that if we take the time for meditation, we end up having more time, not less at the end of our day. We give it a try for its healing power. We try one thing at a time not so much because we need it but because we deserve it.

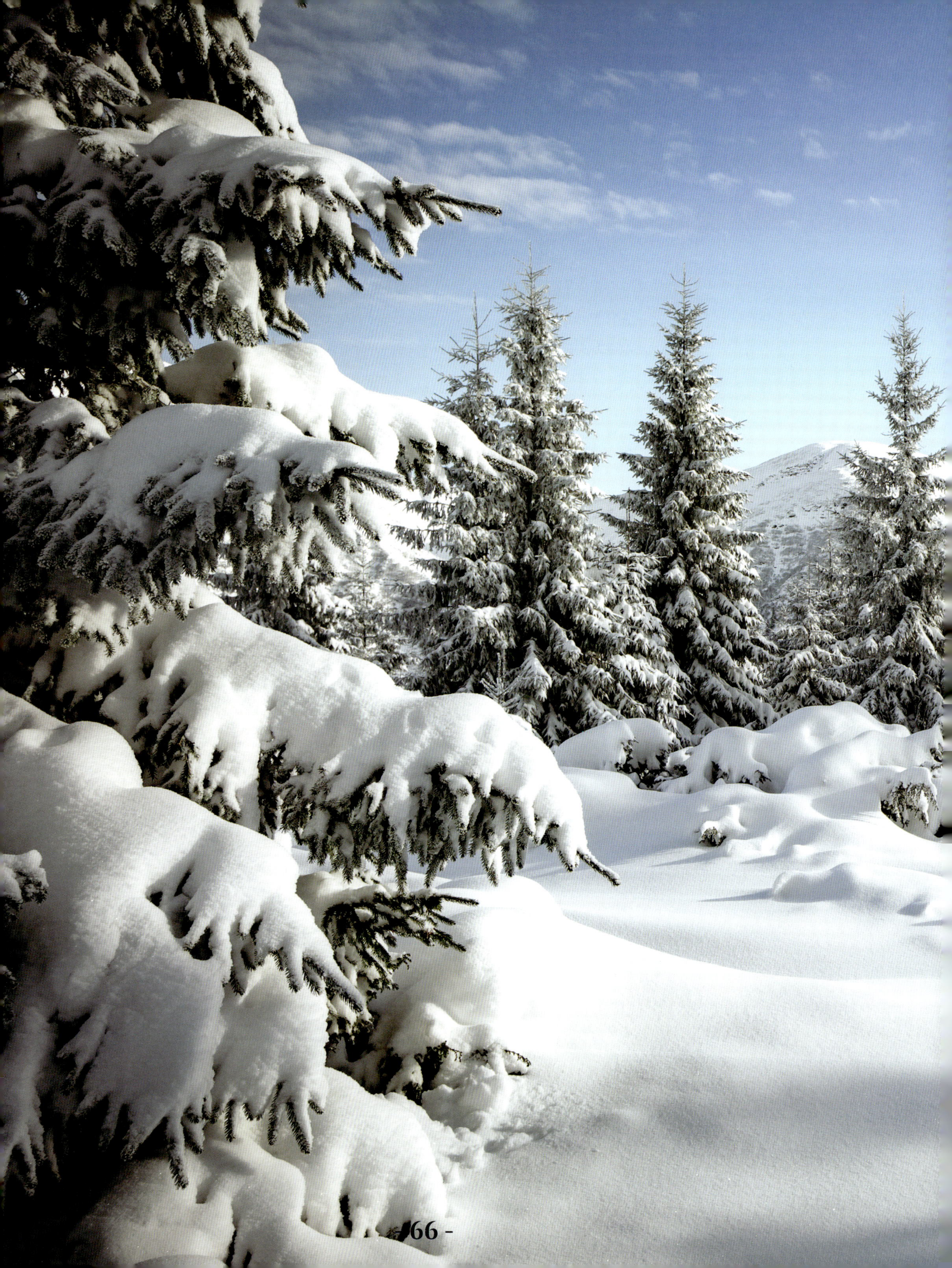

JANUARY

During this season of resolutions, we learn to keep promises at bay. We make our plans but we no longer plan outcomes. We try to remain healthy in the present so the future can take care of itself. We take each day as it comes. We resolve only to listen more carefully as our hearts stay strong like evergreens in blankets of snow. Who are the people our experience will help in this coming year? Some will be family, some old friends and, of course, some complete strangers. The beginning of a new year does not automatically call for a giant to-do list for the coming time. It is, however, a time to recall the endurance we've always had and to be reminded that, like great pines in drifts of snow, we will stand invincible against the cold.

AFFIRMATION This month I won't get caught up in elaborate plans or promises. I will live in each day and take the best of each day. I will appreciate the challenges of each day by giving to those challenges my heart and my will. It's not easy but even in the cold, I know the evergreens stand tall …and I will survive. I will survive.

MY WISHES FOR JANUARY _____

_____

_____

_____

Seasons of Feeling

FEBRUARY

In the horizon is our hope. And the world is rich with people just like us, who need friendship and care. We find fulfillment in helping others navigate the rocky way of grief. This month could be a call to think about what we can do to make a difference in the life of a family member, a friend or some other needy soul we may encounter. The sun is readying itself to pierce the clouds and though we comb the shore with wounded hearts, there are still places to go, horizons to seek.

AFFIRMATION This month I will seek outlets for my love and compassion. I will look for the beauty of the sunset when I find it. Even the rocky trials of my life can be of use. This month I will give to others more consciously and put my trust in my own capacity for love.

MY WISHES FOR FEBRUARY _____

_____

_____

_____

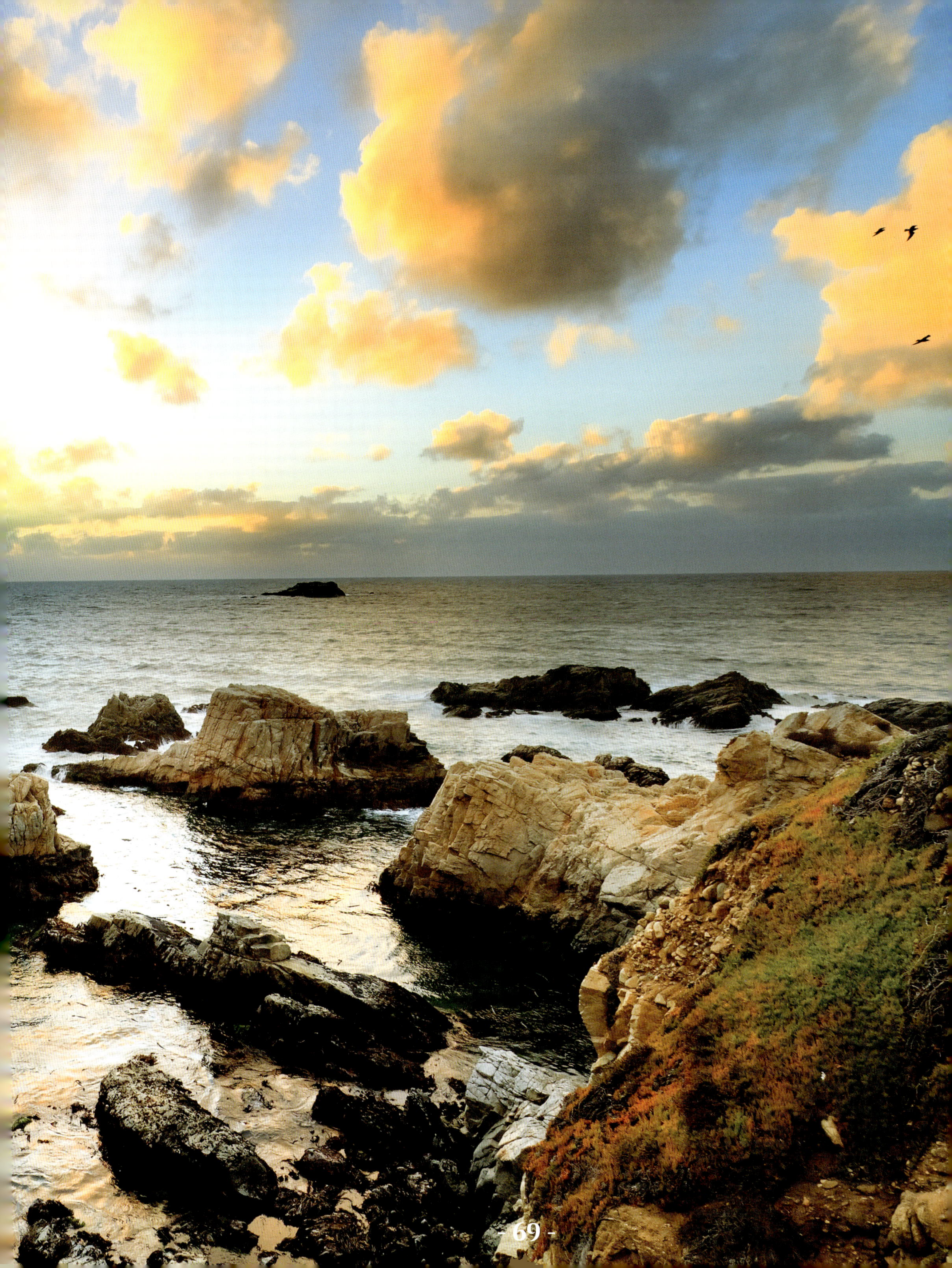

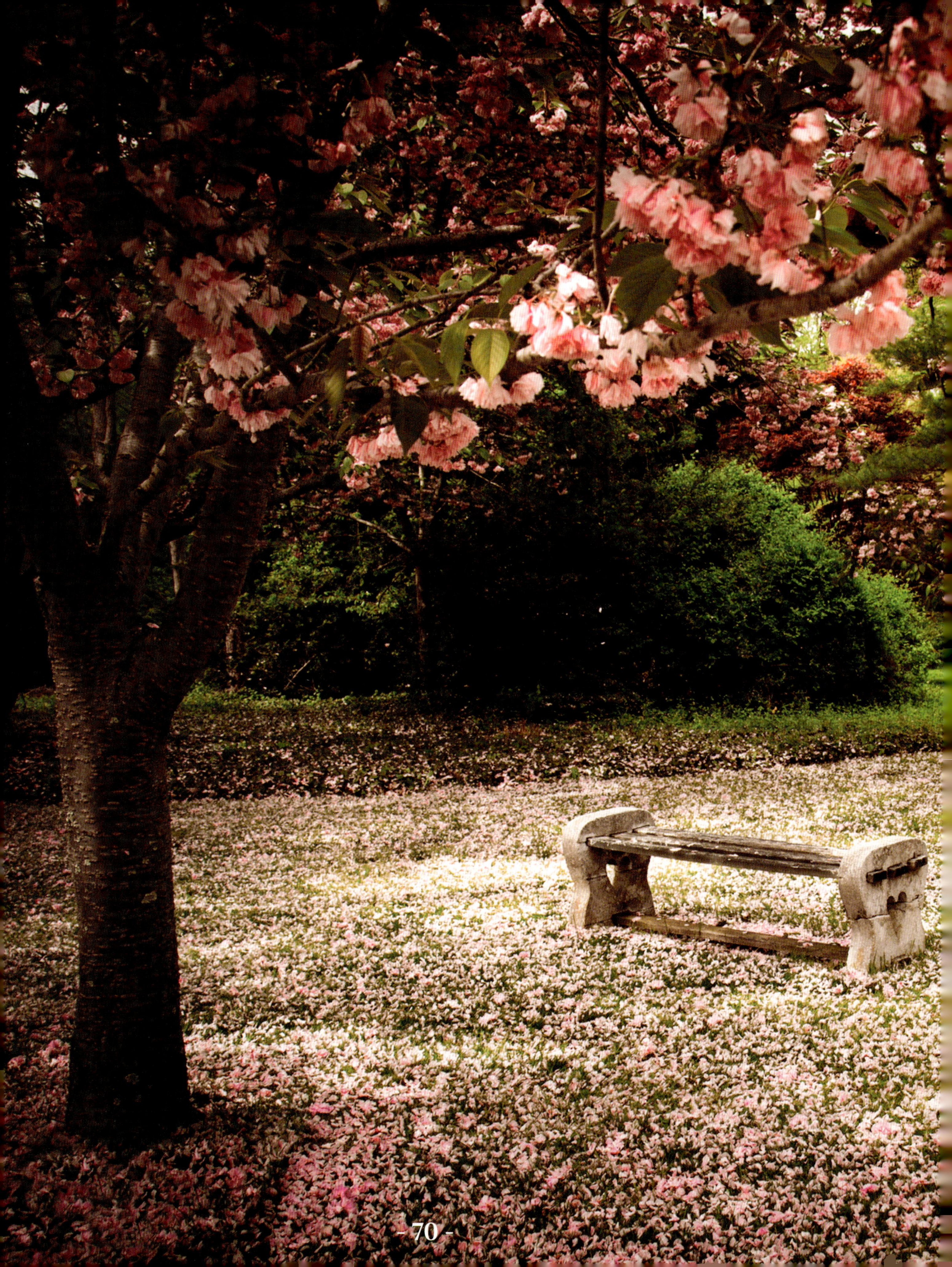

Seasons of Feeling

MARCH

As winter winds itself down we look to new growth. We are all a bit frightened of the unknown, but new blossoms are stewn beautifully about the landscape. So many helped us get this far. We see a new life surrounding us and we continue to rely on the goodness of people close to us. It is no weakness to call for help; indeed sometimes it is a sign of strength and maturity. So as we go about the early spring we make sure there is room for those who continue to be by our side. There will be times they will need us, too. And we hope to be able to be present for them as they have been for us.

AFFIRMATION This month I am going to find a way to show my gratitude to those who have stayed close to me in rough waters. It's usually the little things that are so meaningful, and there are a lot of little things I can do to quietly show my sincere gratitude to the good people around me.

MY WISHES FOR MARCH _____

_____

_____

_____

Seasons of Feeling

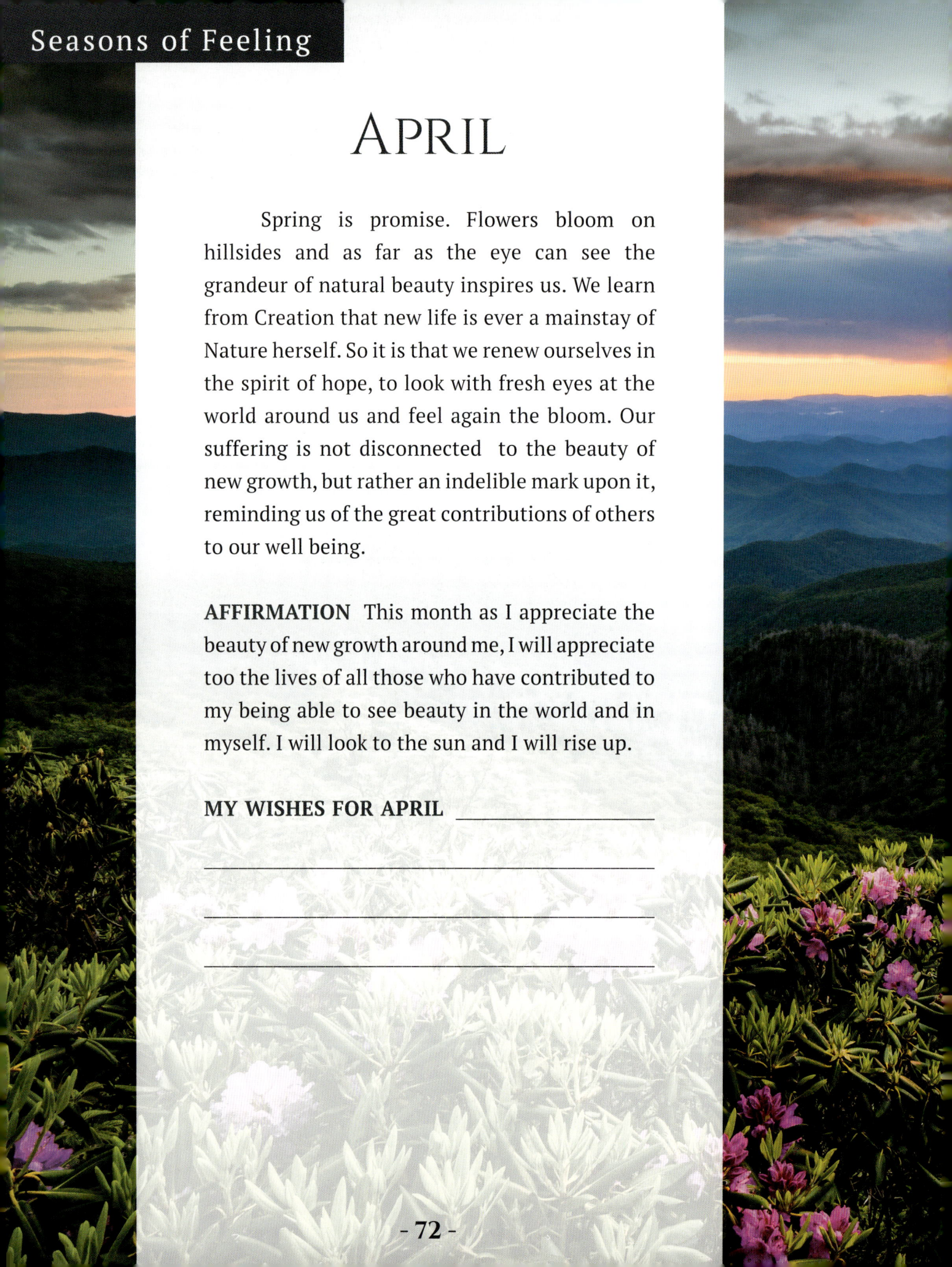

April

Spring is promise. Flowers bloom on hillsides and as far as the eye can see the grandeur of natural beauty inspires us. We learn from Creation that new life is ever a mainstay of Nature herself. So it is that we renew ourselves in the spirit of hope, to look with fresh eyes at the world around us and feel again the bloom. Our suffering is not disconnected to the beauty of new growth, but rather an indelible mark upon it, reminding us of the great contributions of others to our well being.

AFFIRMATION This month as I appreciate the beauty of new growth around me, I will appreciate too the lives of all those who have contributed to my being able to see beauty in the world and in myself. I will look to the sun and I will rise up.

MY WISHES FOR APRIL _____

_____

_____

_____

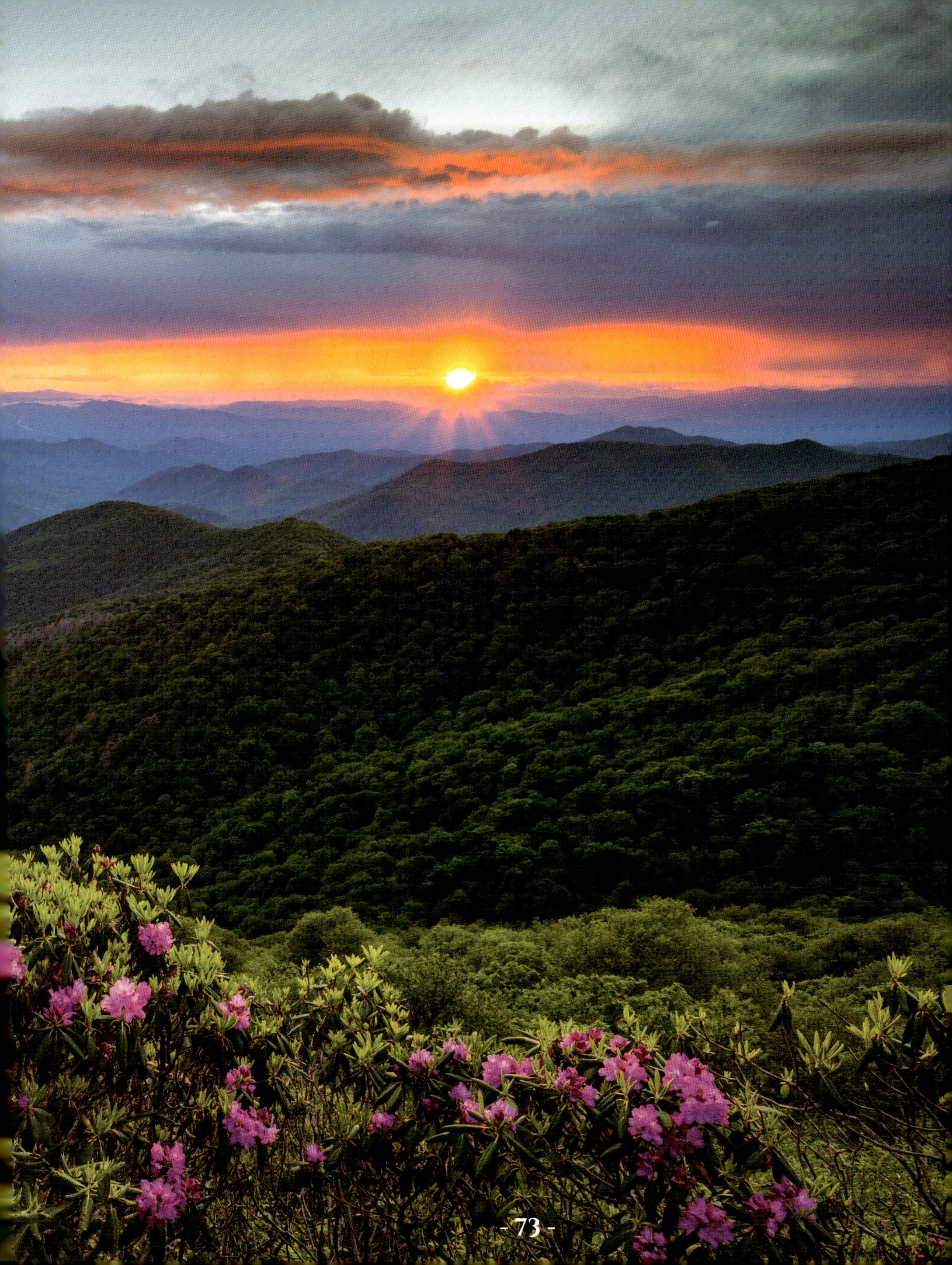

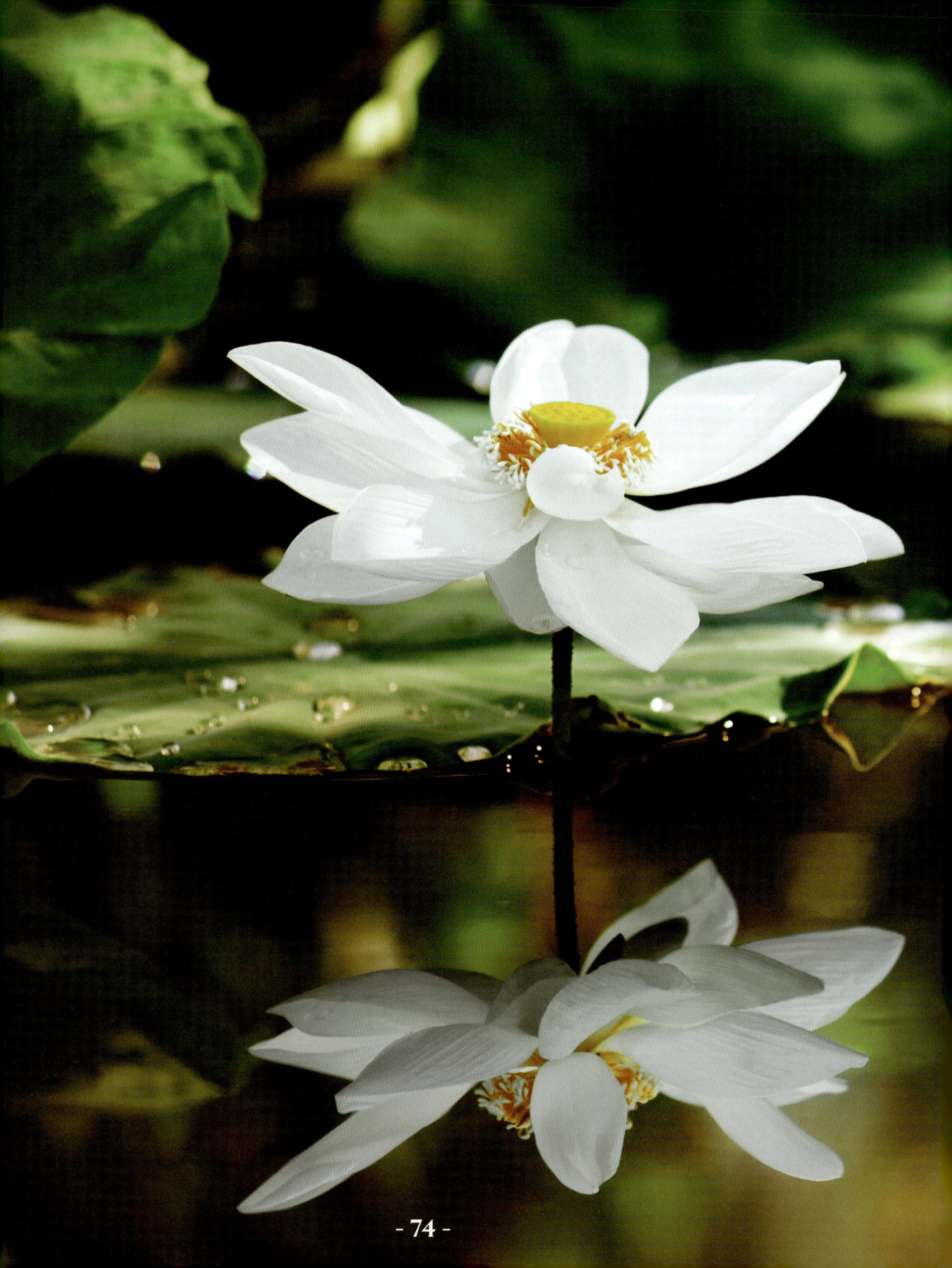

Seasons of Feeling

MAY

Between the cold of winter and the heat of summer is a time of reflection, a time to peer inside ourselves, to see how we have wrestled with our pain, to see how we have positioned ourselves for the inevitable changes life brings our way. There is much to see when we have been wounded by loss. In reflection we look over a pond and the water that has settled there and the beauty that floats about it. Life settles in; it is punctuated by sadness as it is by joy. Though the pond is mystery, we peer down upon the goodness a life has generated. And once we have done this, our own reflection abides in that goodness.

AFFIRMATION This month I will reflect upon the goodness of my loved one and beauty in the pond of my life. I will not only cherish the memory of that goodness; I will incorporate it into my daily living. Though I falter and succumb to fear and loneliness, I keep on going because the goodness enlivens me over and over again. This month I will give in to the goodness that I find upon reflection.

MY WISHES FOR MAY _____

_____

_____

_____

Seasons of Feeling

JUNE

Grief is like the great depth of the mysterious sea meeting the shoreline of our lives. There is so much we can't see; so much we don't know. But the waning sun, the tall grasses, the white sand underfoot all give us comfort. In June the seaside can lead us back to thoughts of childhood when families wandered off together and kids dug for shells in the idleness youth affords. Though we cannot recapture those days and that time, let us try to appreciate the coming of summer with a more childlike acceptance of the losses we have endured and the triumphs we have enjoyed. There is a bittersweet warmth where the sea meets the shore.

AFFIRMATION This month I will imagine the gifts of childhood try to let myself experience the resiliency that a child experiences. There is an innocence that may help me find strength for my difficulties and direction for my sorrow and my joy.

MY WISHES FOR JUNE _____

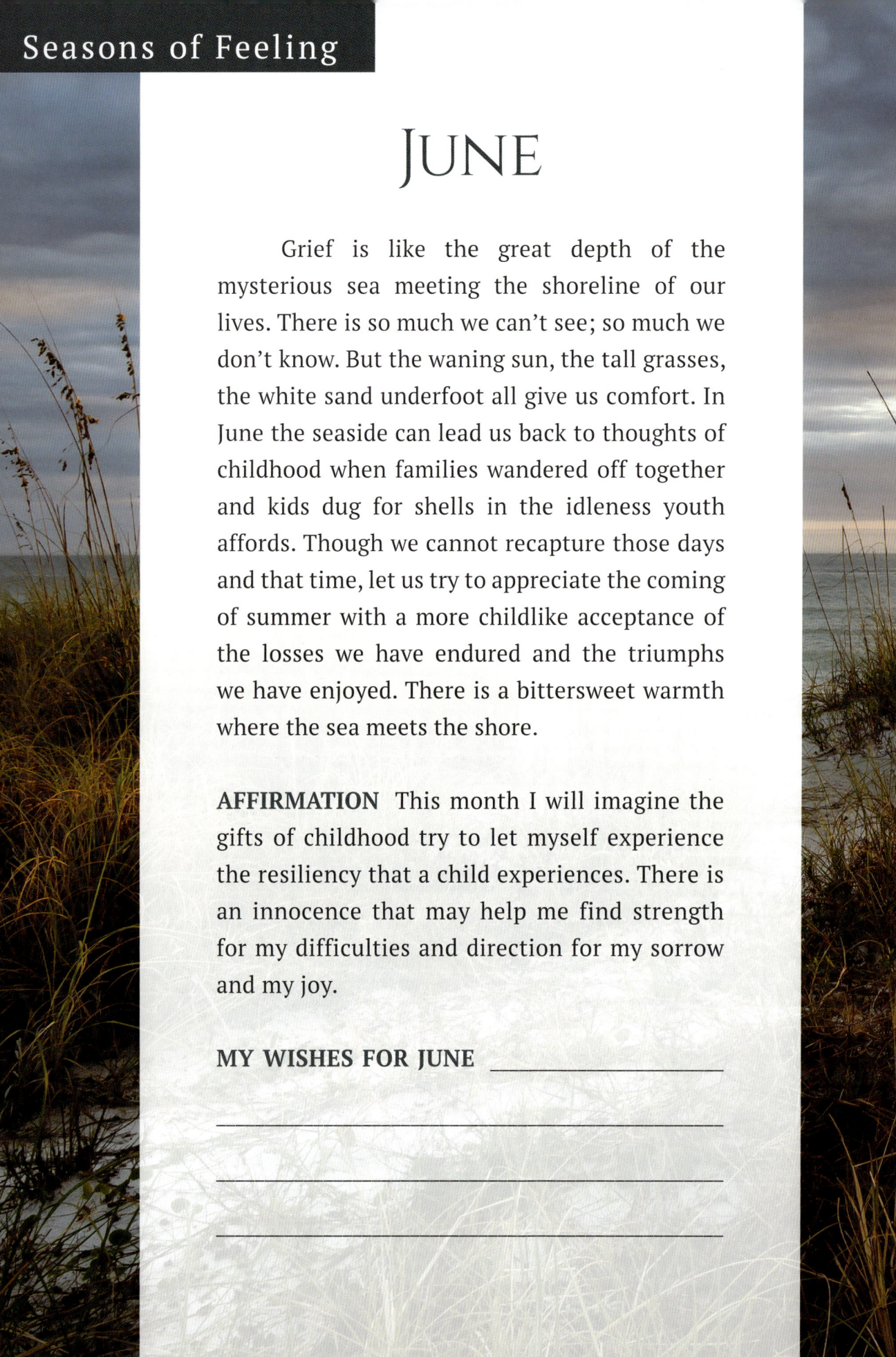

_____

_____

_____

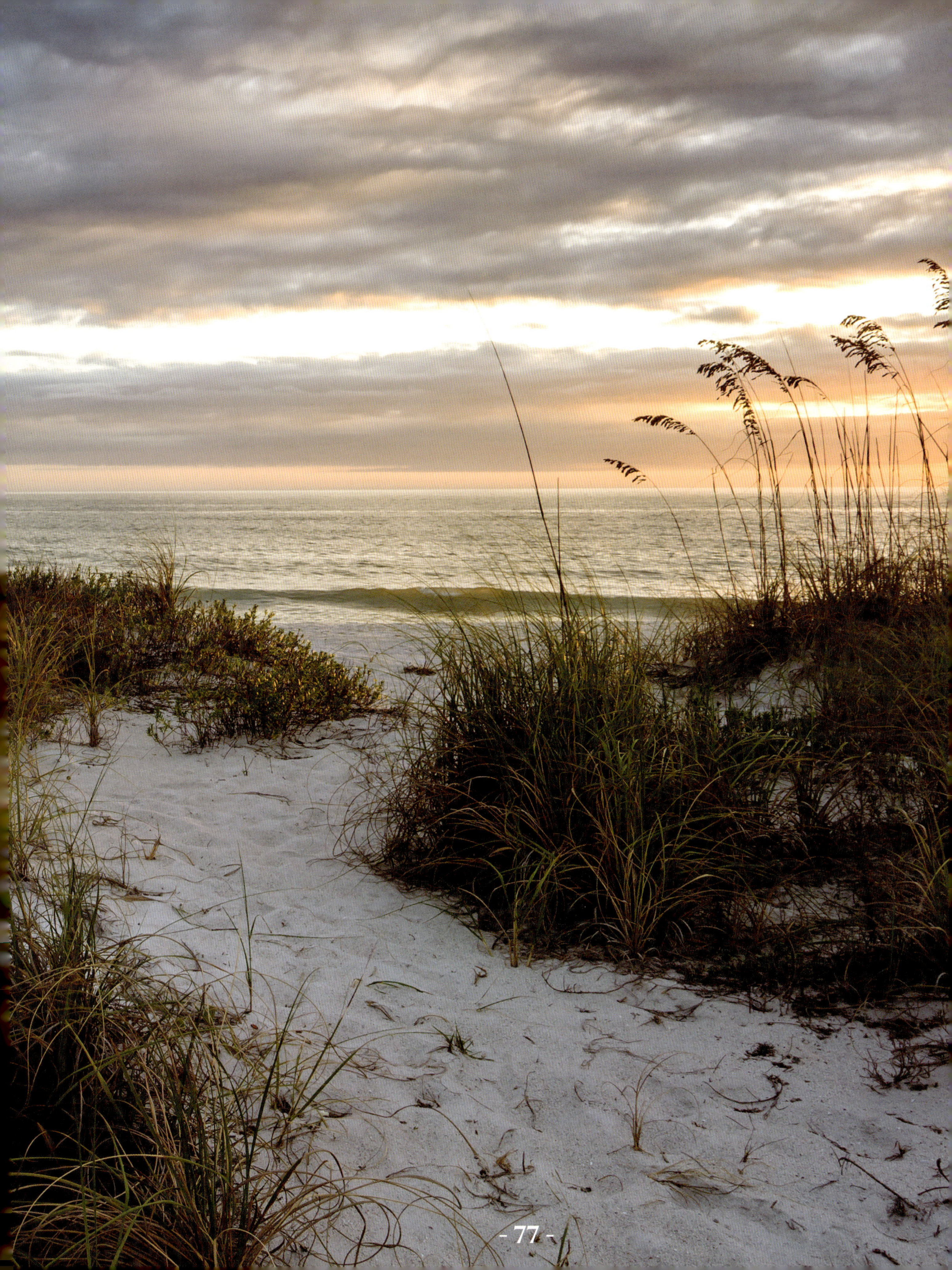

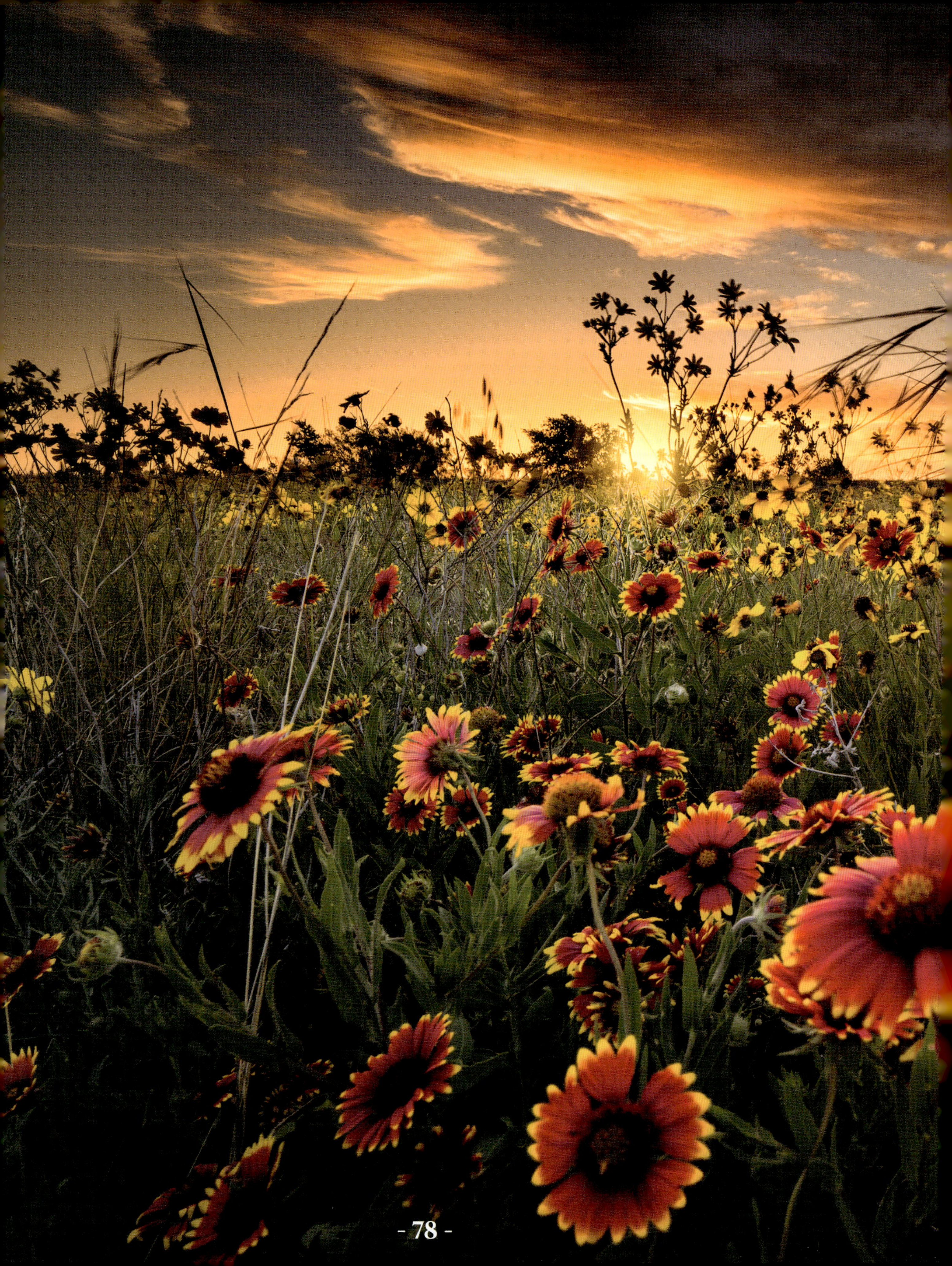

Seasons of Feeling

JULY

What we really celebrate when we celebrate our independence as a country is our interdependence on each other as citizens. True independence is a by-product of appropriate interdependencies among people who care about each other. We are wildflowers strewn among other wildflowers, groups of people defined by what they love and hold in common... communities. Here we find our support in times of grief and sorrow. We are grateful to the American community for our freedom, as we are grateful to the various communities of citizens with whom we share our lives.

AFFIRMATION This month I will take time to reflect upon the treasure that is my country. I will also demonstrate to the people I call neighbors, that is, my community, my gratitude for their on going support. This month I will attempt to further cultivate a "community spirit".

MY WISHES FOR JULY _____

_____

_____

_____

Seasons of Feeling

AUGUST

Grief can be as draining as the lingering heat of summer. All our energy is expelled just to keep going and what beauty lies ahead we do not see. A vista, a vision of tomorrow, ancient hills stretching out in the distance may let us know that, just as death absorbs us, so too does life roll out before us. A breeze, a stone wall, a slice of sunlight might be just the thing to provide a little relief and regeneration. We look for the respite that comes from beauty. The vista may be a friend, the vision an activity like a church or grief support group. And the hills our family waiting for us in the setting of the sun. All of us, bereaved or not, need beauty and life affirming experiences with people we care for.

AFFIRMATION This month I will consciously look for a way to reconnect with the beauty of fellowship. I will find that the good and the beautiful can help to counteract the weariness of sorrow. I will find a way to relax a little and find time for fellowship, for leisure and for good health.

MY WISHES FOR AUGUST _____

_____

_____

_____

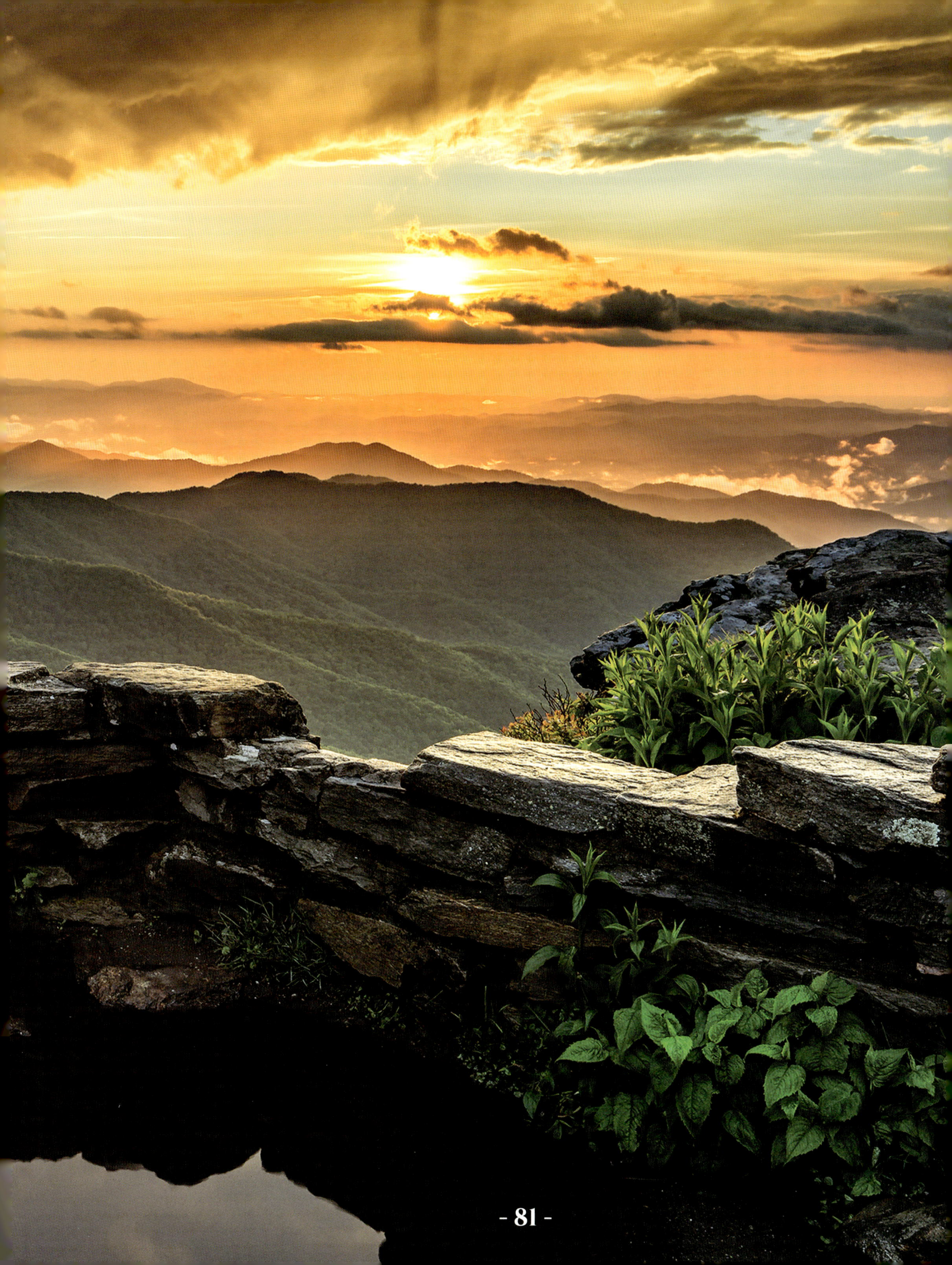

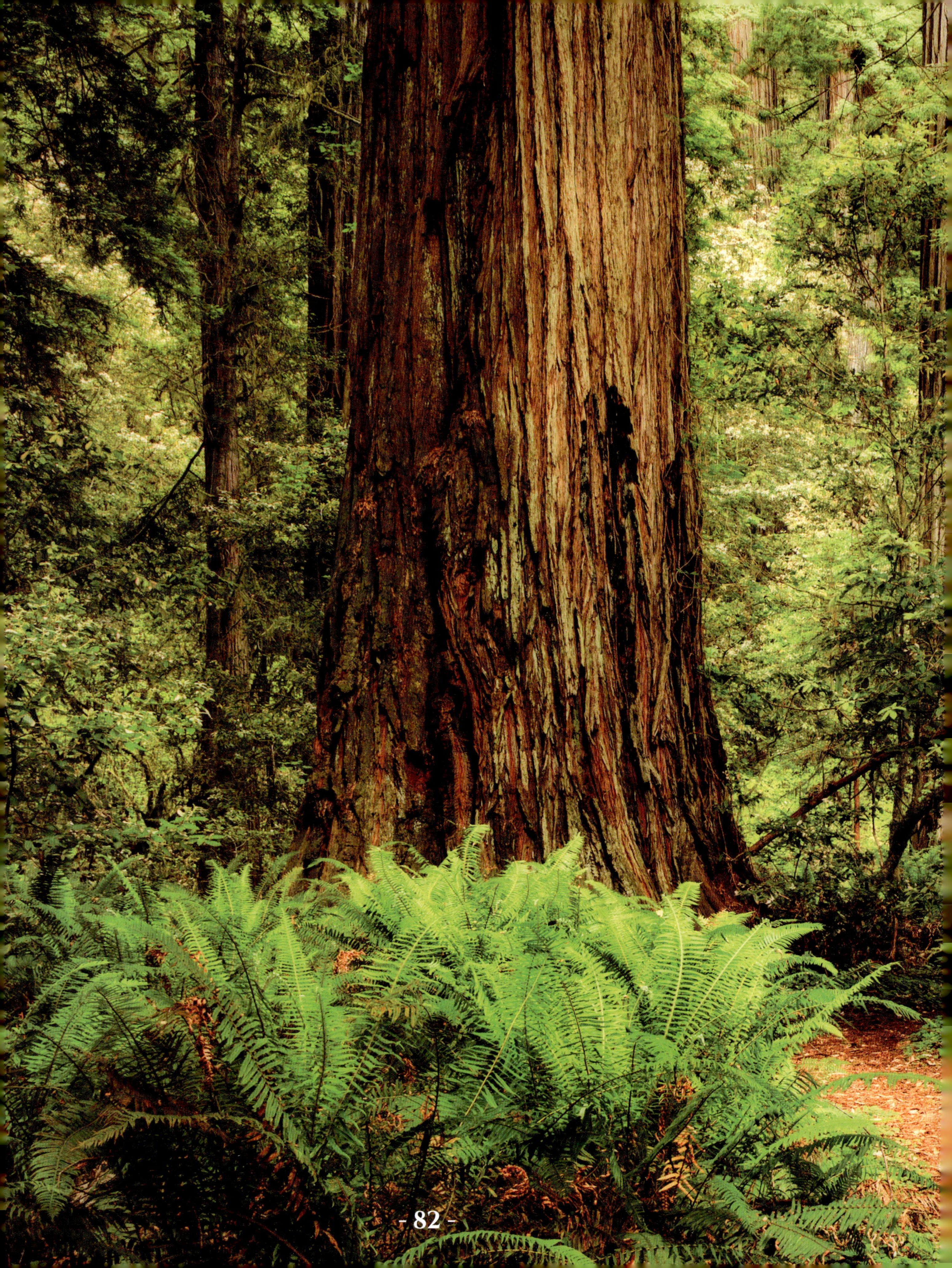

SEPTEMBER

September brings the very particular sensations of fall. The clean, crisp air begins to fill us up with welcome relief from the summer's heat and thoughts that journey back to days gone by. We reflect upon the past. A melancholy sometimes comes, a longing for the people and situations that used to give us such joy. There is nothing unnatural about these thoughts. We let them come and we let them go. Our thoughts are a forest of foliage and trees; our moods turn like the leaves. We let nature color our world as it keeps our depression at bay. We allow nature to run her course through us in peace and understanding.

AFFIRMATION This month I will observe the constancy and beauty of the natural world as I appreciate the joys of yesterday and the hope for tomorrow. I will let Mother Nature speak to me gently and with her abounding wisdom. I will venture out into the freshness of the beginning of a new season, admitting and accepting my sorrow as I cultivate hope and the promise of new and better days ahead.

MY WISHES FOR SEPTEMBER _____

_____

_____

_____

Seasons of Feeling

OCTOBER

This month, even in the midst of change, Mother Nature flaunts her brilliance. And yet, it seems that everywhere we look are remnants of a life gone by, the heartfelt and lovely vestiges of another life. Like the presence of an old creek side mill, there is an archive of beauty in our own hearts and all around that remembered past is a radiance of color and feeling. It is a part of the landscape of our lives now. And with the help of so many of our loved ones, alive or not, we appreciate the bright moments that have enriched us along the way.

AFFIRMATION This month I will honor my past, all I have given and all I have received. I will seek to understand more how my own history might be repurposed to aid others. Before me, now, trees are lit with the cycle of their beauty. And there is beauty yet left for me to experience. This month, as I pay tribute to the past and those with whom I have shared my life, I will also witness to the power and the beauty of the human spirit.

MY WISHES FOR OCTOBER _____

_____

_____

_____

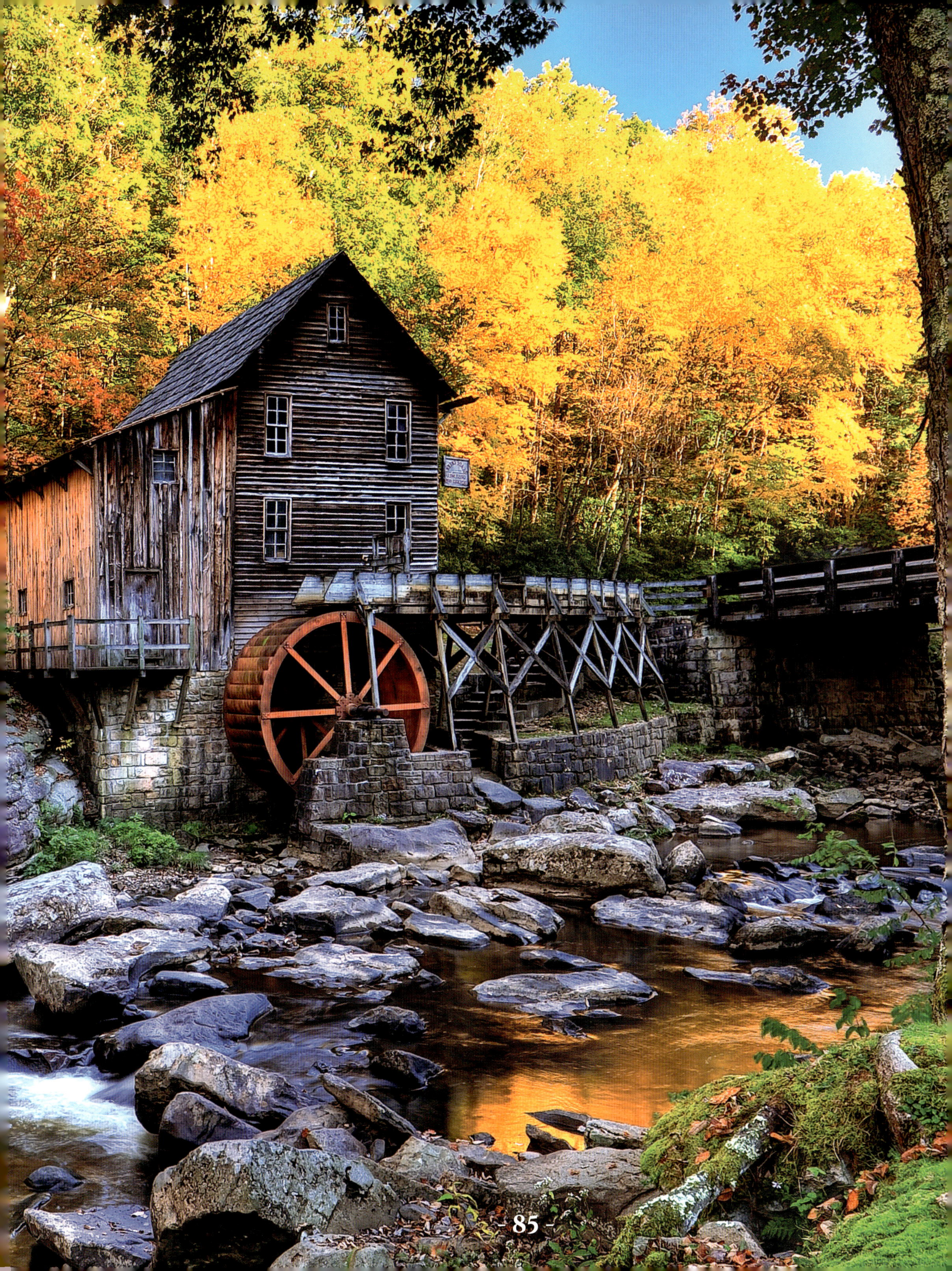

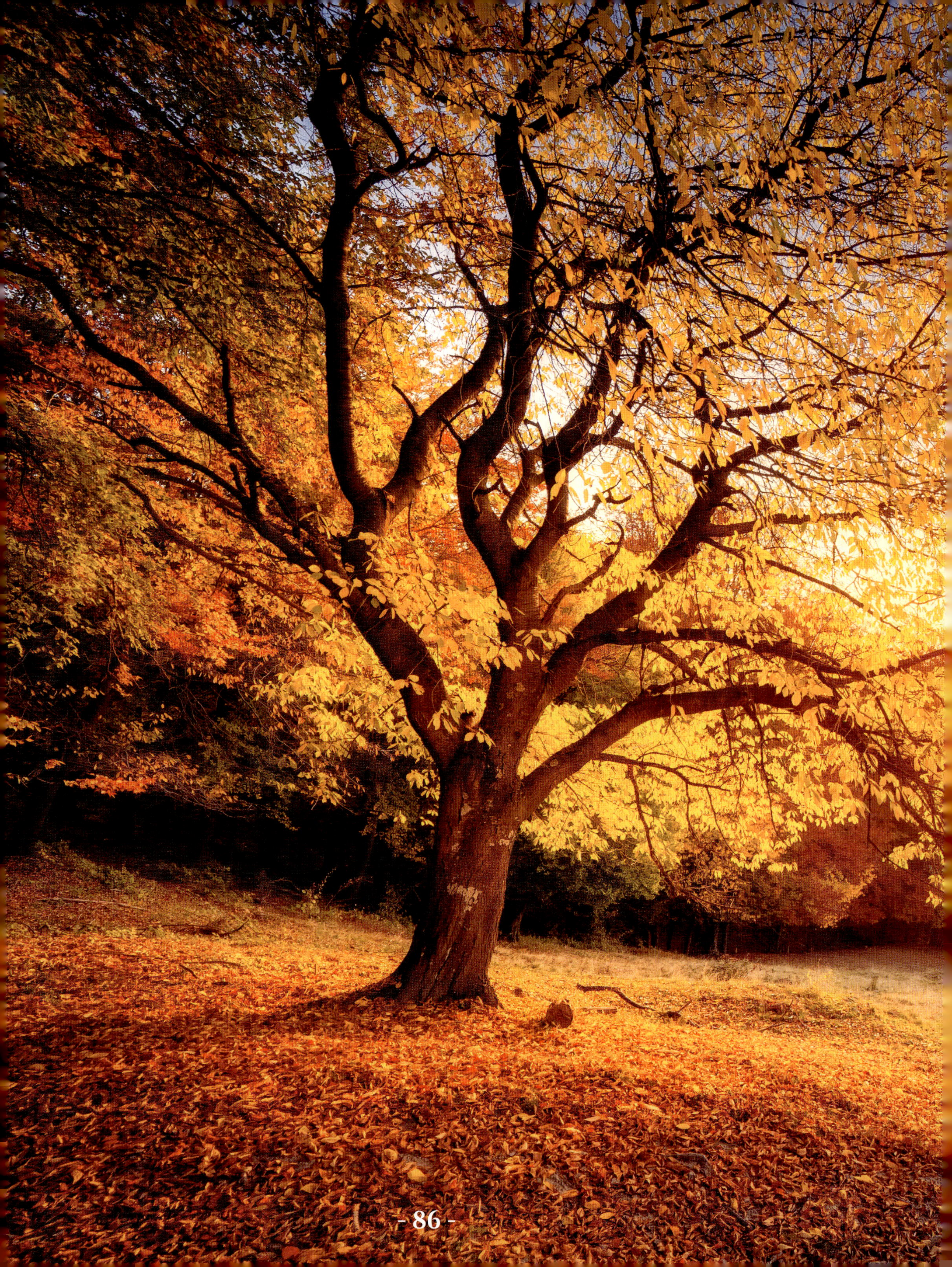

NOVEMBER

This month we give thanks for the land that has nurtured us and the people who have been a part of our lives. We step back and look at our many blessings. Our country has often stood like a lone tree as a refuge and a protector, her limbs and her radiance reaching out to citizens like a friend or family member. As we gather with friends or family over a Thanksgiving meal, or if we honor the day alone, this is also a good time to count our personal blessings, even as we struggle with the pain of loss. Even in the loss of a dear loved one we can see the blessing of having been a part of their life.

AFFIRMATION This month I will remind myself of my many blessings. I will meditate on what it is to live the span of one's life in a free country. I hope I can somehow show my gratitude for our nation and for the very special people who have been a part of my life.

MY WISHES FOR NOVEMBER _____

_____

_____

_____

Seasons of Feeling

Seasons of Feeling

DECEMBER

In the mad consumerism that has come to represent the holiday season, we must find a way to recall and revive genuine friendship and generosity. We have suffered greatly this year and no material gifts can mitigate our pain. But in the icy ridges of our walk we find footprints in the snow that tell us others have trod where we do now. This holiday season perhaps we retreat from the madness and give of our selves to those we love and to those less fortunate than we are. Yes, holidays are tough on the grief-stricken; there is no way around it. But perhaps this is a time to slow the pace for our own good and for the ultimate good of those we know and love.

AFFIRMATION This month, as a gift to my loved ones, those here with me and those deceased, I will have a saner holiday, concentrated on people I care about and not on "things". My real gift to those around me will be my *presence* instead of my presents!

MY WISHES FOR DECEMBER _____

_____

_____

_____

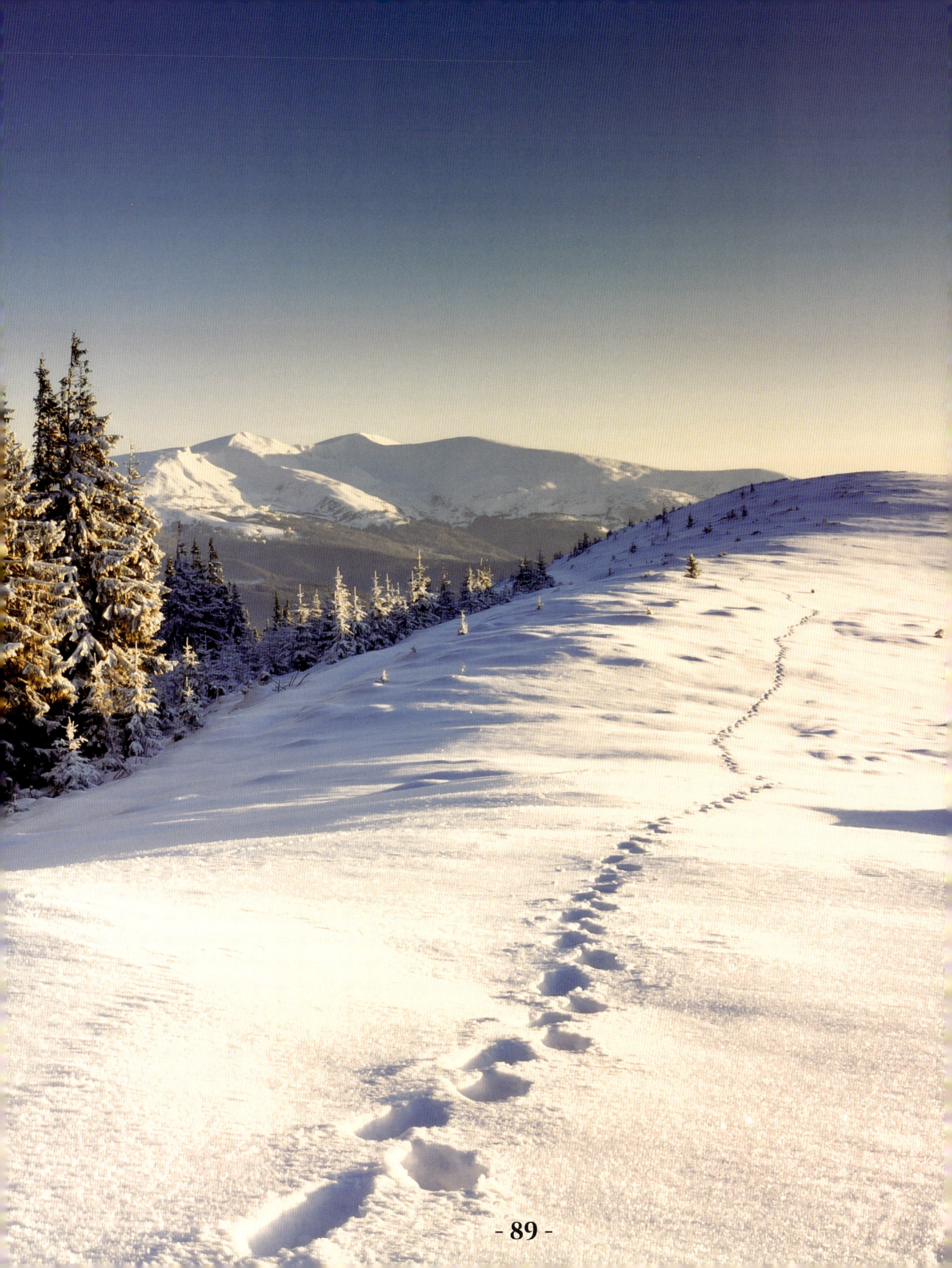

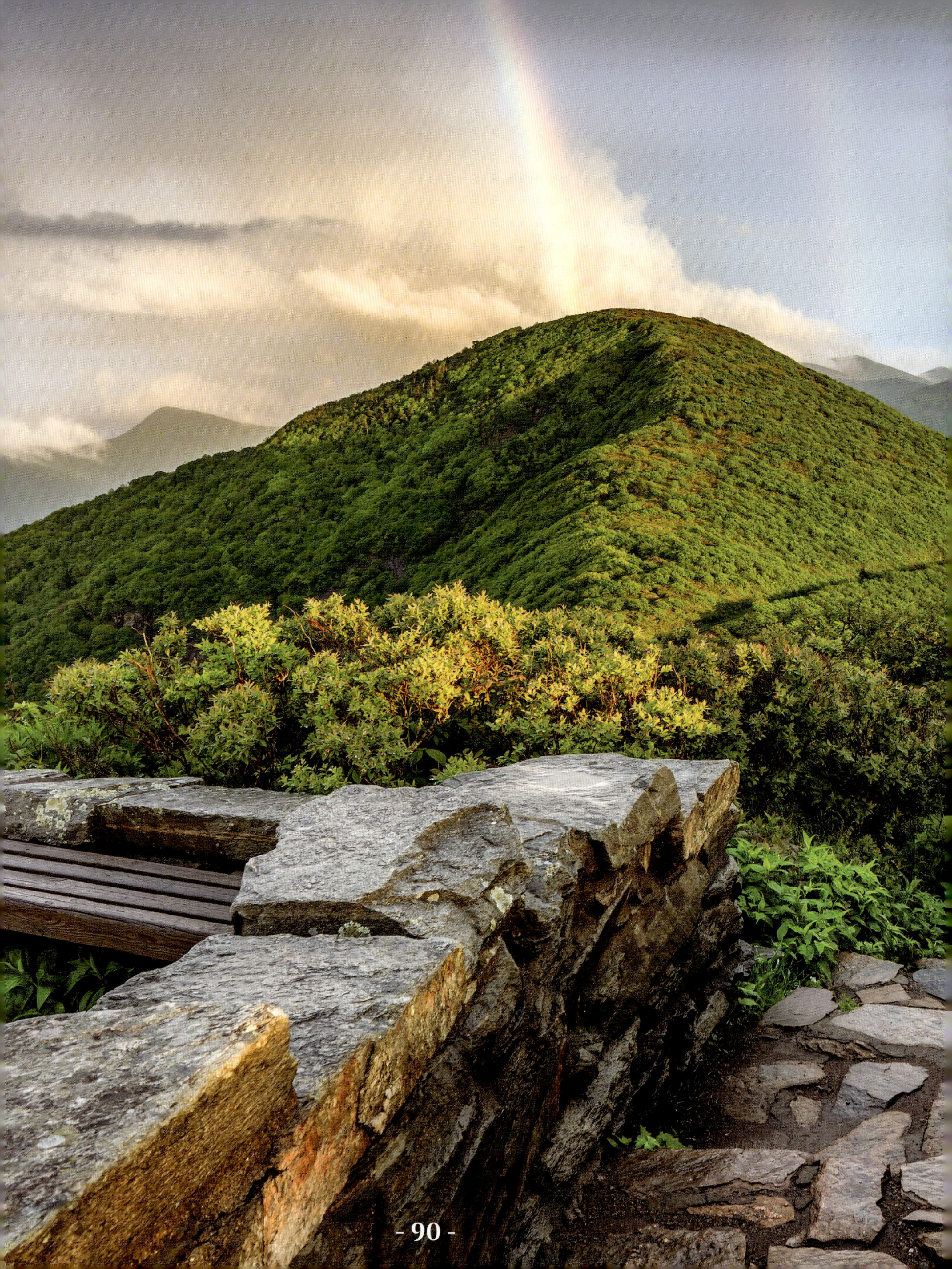

Special Times During the Year

There are occasions: birthdays, holidays, anniversaries, times of the year that were especially meaningful to us that echo through our lives, recalling moments with our loved one that reflected our deepest affection and love. Just as our grieving is tempered by these times so too should these times, as they recur, honor our grief. And as these occasions recur we are made aware, sometimes strikingly, of a wound that still exists, a wound that lets us know our hearts are still alive and that our loved ones still live and abide there. There is no easy way to make it through these special times. The emptiness wants to return and sometimes we are taken aback by the force of our recurring anguish. We thought we had made more progress or walked farther along the path of our bereavement. But the power of the attachment to a loved one now gone becomes ever more evident when we come upon the special times that still have great meaning to us.

When these times are upon us, perhaps it might be good to ask ourselves exactly what it is our minds and hearts are revisiting. Is it not, at least in part, a goodness inherent in the relationship, a closeness that we are better people for having been a part of? Many true celebrations of life are tinged with sadness. The great joy at the birth of a child in the family often causes us to reflect upon those not present. When we celebrate a holiday we also naturally think of those family members unable to be with us. The existence of any great love presupposes the hurt that is a part of that love. Time will help us integrate our loss into the special times of our continuing life. Somehow, during these times, we learn to live with a joy tinged with the wistful longing for one who changed us and still has a unique and beautiful place in our hearts.

Special Times

THE BIRTHDAYS

Birthdays are celebrations of life. The birthdays of our family members are dates we live with, the archived numbers of our personal histories. They represent special moments tucked away in the folds of memory, memory that may come to life in new and surprising ways, especially in the first year after the death of our loved one. As in any life, some memories we may turn from, but many we invite into our hearts to the extent that we are willing and able to do so. When a wish is made and a candle is blown out the lovely smoke still rises and lingers in the air, billowy and wistful and sometimes long into the future. It is a presence that may feel like our hearts are breaking all over again. We are actually grateful our loved ones are still present within us… but we miss them so.

AN AFFIRMATION

I will never forget this birthday. It brings back so many memories. It also brings with it pangs of sorrow and nostalgia. I am homesick for my loved one's presence. Tomorrow will be easier but it is not tomorrow. It is this very day, the one etched in my memory, the one I will forever honor; the one I will recognize for the happiness it once engendered, for the great yearly celebration of the life of one I have loved.

Special Times

THE ANNIVERSARIES

We take note of our wedding days; of the dates we met the special people of our lives, of dates that represent our life changes. We remember them and they become indelible marks upon our minds and our hearts. After our loved one's death, when these days come up we can't help that our minds go back to the good times and the relationship that shared them. The anniversary of our loved one's death is especially difficult, however, and fills us with emotion and powerful memories. These times can be sad times, times of remorse returned, times of silent contemplation. We recognize that we still hurt; we may seek someone close or we may sit alone in our thoughts. We may recall a day when vows were proclaimed, a day when we made other profoundly important decisions, or the last day of a special life. We will also recognize that those days and the images that accompany them, serve as a memorial to our loved one, forever and ever.

AN AFFIRMATION

I sit with my memories and they are good. But they remind me of how much I miss the one I love. What a day to remember. I remember so many details. Those details are a part of who I am. I am glad they are there and I am glad my heart is full, even if it hurts. Today I will remember how the little things of a life well-lived build a network of experience that makes me grateful for my life and grateful for the loved ones who have been a part of it.

Special Times

THE HOLIDAYS

Holidays: Thanksgiving, Christmas, Easter, July 4th, and others are always special. And now, with a death in the family, they remain special, but in a different way. Christmas especially tugs at our heartstrings and can get downright depressing because the person we shared the season with is no longer here. Perhaps we buy or make a memorial tree ornament or place a special remembrance in a stocking. We might share with someone close the difficulty in making it through the holidays. We may just wait it out or even figure out some new way to make the best of it. Holidays following the loss of a loved one can become the height of loneliness, especially in the first year. Some trudge through it, some withdraw, some put on a happy face and try to extract something from the joy of others. However we deal with the holidays, we place our own stamp on them. They will come to mean more as time goes on; now in this first year, they only seem to remind us of the absence in our lives. But that very absence also reminds us of the presence in our hearts.

AN AFFIRMATION

The holidays are here and I know it will be a hard time. I will be aware of the subtleties of the season as never before because my senses are sharpened and even, at times, raw. And just as the wind, biting and frigid, seems to blow through me, I am aware of the joy of others. I recall the best of our own holiday times, grateful that I and my loved one had them, grateful that we believed in them and that we gave ourselves to celebrations of life. I will, deep in my heart, celebrate yet.

Special Times

THE ANNIVERSARIES OF A DEATH

The date we lose a loved one will be etched into our memory. We remember: a face at a bedside, a hospital hallway, our loved one's hands, the tears of a relative, the condolences of a friend. We pack the memories away the best we can; we continue to grieve; we carry on. And then, all too soon, the anniversary of the death arrives and we are surprised how clear the memories are and how deeply we still feel pangs of sorrow. When we say we'll never get over a loved one's passing we mean simply that we are changed; we mean that a life has affected us profoundly. This anniversary we may explore our gratitude for life itself or we may ask once again, "Why?" And somewhere deep inside we have found out in this last year that our answer comes in the living out of our own lives, day by day. We know that love, indeed, never ends. It lives even beyond all the special times of remembrance; it lives beyond this very day.

AN AFFIRMATION

This is a tough day to get through. I am flooded with memories of bits and pieces of a life and a loss. How do I express what these images mean to me? Can I draw a picture or write a poem? Can I play notes on a piano that touch my heart in recognition or might I be able to speak with a friend who understands? Might I find a quiet place to let the feelings come and go? It is a tough day, no way around it. But it is my day. I claim it in honor of the love between me and my departed loved one. I miss our time together and today I want others to know how deep love can be. I will find a way to express that… just as I have found a way to live.

WINTER

The fine first snow does slowly fall
    and shivering arms cross in the cold.
We see there now a young one's breath,
    we huddle close to mind our old.
Winter chills our hearts and souls
    for someone close has died.
And memories of that singular life
    we warmed with love and cried.
And from now on we make our way
    in drifts of ice and snow,
unsure of footing in our turns
    but knowing what we know:
that death is but the turn of life
    the leaves that fall, the streams that flow.
Though arms will cross in wind and cold
    we keep in mind below
a greener life hides underneath
    the mystery of the snow.

SPRING

When the moon is high
    and jonquils rise
and a lonesome, lustrous
    shower cries;
starlings will return
    to their rooftops soon
and the pear, the cherry
    and the dogwoods bloom;
when dusk, serene
    and silent as death
makes of evening
    a sacred breath,
dusk a lavish
    refuge dear;
we know then the spring
    of the year is here.

SUMMER

The summer never seems to know
   that death is by her side
that we just lost a loved one,
   that now we must abide.
The sunlight chases after us;
   it chases us outdoors.
We cease to look at empty rooms;
   we open up our doors.
We walk along the fences now
   where sunlight plays its games,
where youngsters run and climb and laugh
   and shout each others' names.
They roam the grassy hills of home
   and think not of death or sorrow
while we lean on rails and watch them
   as they signify tomorrow.
We walk the fields and shadows
   with sadness in the summer's sun.
But our lovely balm is children there
   who are dancing where the fences run.

FALL

The autumn calls our hearts to home
    To blush and twilight views,
to early evening memories
    and early morning dews.
What does it mean when chills are here
    when air is crisp and clean?
When those who leave us leave us now
    what does their absence mean?
We know our love sways not to ground;
    it dances in the air.
Our loved ones live within us still;
    they sing and laugh and care.
Remember in the fall of year
    the ones we got to know,
the ones who stole our hearts away
    the ones who helped us grow.
Remember in the fall of year
    the fields that call us home,
the loved one who lives in us still...
    no, we are not alone.

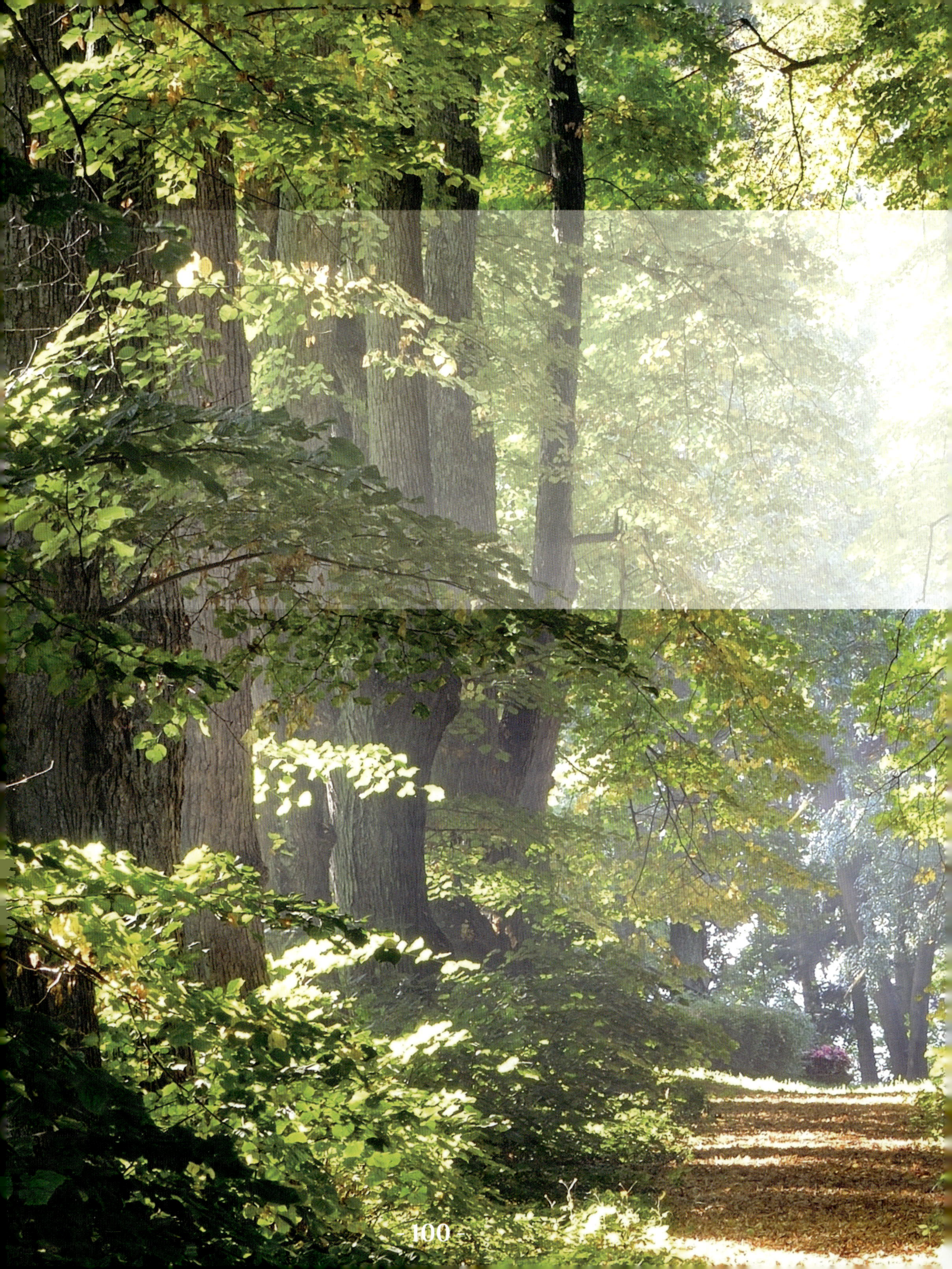

PART FOUR
The Way of Hope

"Pursue some path, however narrow and crooked, in which you can walk with love and reverence."
— Henry David Thoreau

Resource Section

Helpful Bereavement Resources

*We cannot live only for ourselves.
A thousand fibers connect us with our fellow men.
—Herman Melville*

In the following pages we have provided a list of things that may have to be done in the weeks and months following the funeral of your loved one. You will encounter certain key responsibilities in that time and it is paramount to remember you are not alone! Help is available and slowly but surely the tasks will get done. We have also listed some websites, books and organizations that may be of help to you. They represent a bare few of the resources available and some will be more appropriate than others. But all represent an effort to reach out to you in the sadness and sorrow you live with at the present time.

In our grieving books can play an important role when we read about what others have experienced and about practical ways to cope with what has happened in our lives or when we read of the resiliency of the human spirit and of a better time coming. We have listed a handful of books that may provide a measure of consolation and hope.

You will also find listed organizations dedicated to helping individuals in their grief. They may specialize in one or another grief related issues or they may be a general store of information, empathy and practical ways to cope with the loss of a loved one. A brief list is provided here.

And of course today few of us are very far from a computer and through the internet handy information on just about any topic is right at our fingertips. In that spirit, we have provided just a few websites specific to grief and the grieving process. Many of these sites represent a community of people who have gathered to share some of the most compelling lessons of a lifetime.

Resource Section

WHAT NOW?

Surrounding the death of a loved one there are a number of practical matters to which we must attend. We have already notified immediate family and extended family, perhaps clergy or other helping friends. We have made funeral arrangements and obtained a death certificate. And what now? What are the other practical matters that will command our attention in the coming days? The following material is intended as a starting point and a reminder of some of the things we wish we didn't have to tend to but that exist nonetheless. Some require an immediate response and others can wait. Having the tasks laid out before us might just help when taking those first necessary steps.

THIS IS CERTAINLY NOT AN EXHAUSTIVE LIST. One of the keys to tending to the various responsibilities following a death in the family is the willingness to ask for help. With the right kind of aid we may come to see the daunting tasks before us as, at the very least, manageable and it is good to remember that those who will be helping us are often honored to contribute to our well-being in such a personal manner. Any of those whose help we enlist will of course be people we have known for a long time and trust implicitly with any aspect of our life. Unfortunately, there are individuals of dubious character that prey on the bereaved, especially the senior citizens amongst us. We understand how very important it is to know and trust the people with whom we are seeking help or advice.

Resource Section

AFTER THE FUNERAL

It can be a quite daunting task to begin taking care of all the practical things that need to be done. Our local funeral director is certainly familiar with issues surrounding a death in the family and may well be able to point us in the right direction.

Our lawyer will deal with matters pertaining to our loved one's will, such as the filing in probate court and the settling of all attendant matters. Whether there is a will or not, the lawyer will also be involved in any appropriate estate expenses or disbursements. If there are any trust agreements the lawyer will help in understanding them as well.

We also make sure to consult with our lawyer, CPA or tax consultant concerning any tax issues that will arise.

We will most likely need a number of copies of the death certificate that may be required from insurance companies and others.

If our deceased had power of attorney, that person should be contacted.

Bank accounts and safe deposit boxes need to be switched into the name of the surviving owner.

Of course, household bills must still be paid and creditors notified. In some cases, however, we will find that the estate is the liable entity for some things owed and therefore we are very careful at first about paying creditors from our own pocket. Good legal advice is obviously important in these matters.

Insurance policies will need to be reviewed and in some cases acted upon. These will include life insurance, auto insurance, health insurance, homeowners insurance, etc. We will also be looking at any personal property owned by our deceased and the possible ramifications of our loved one's death on individual or joint ownership of property of any sort.

With our loved one's employer we will be speaking with someone in the human resources department to understand the importance of any possible retirement accounts or insurance policies.

Resource Section

A Ritual of Love

Disposing of a loved one's personal items and clothing can be a task of great intimacy and depth of feeling. They are our tasks (or our tasks to delegate if we so desire) and therefore they are accomplished on our own timeline. What we keep, what we throw away and what we give away has real meaning. Sometimes the smallest of items or the seemingly most ordinary can become a treasured keepsake. How we choose to do it can also have a great effect on those around us, especially family and close friends. We may recall mementos from departed family members or friends and we remember how inspiring such gifts can be.

Personal effects are just that: personal. We can smell husband, father or grandfather in his shirt or jacket; wife, mother or grandmother in her blouse or perhaps a favorite scarf. We wince at the sight of a child's jumper or the almost animated shoes of a little one now lost to us. A pocketknife once carried, a brooch once pinned, a watch, a ring, a necklace once worn: the things of a life are intimately connected to the life that was lived. Her favorite shawl, his favorite sweater, something passed on already from an earlier generation, something received not so very long ago: a cherished gift, a unique remembrance. These might be the sacred tokens of familiarity we came to know. And so, what now? What will be of them? We decide. It is perhaps the hardest thing we do following the death in the family. But underneath this sad ritual of separation, we come to see the honor in it, too. We come to see the richness of a life through the things that wove in and out of that life, the "stuff" to which our loved one became attached. This ritual of love is the hardest to accomplish, the most poignant, the most heart wrenching. But it is also the greatest privilege to see in the ordinary things of everyday life hues of goodness and worthy living, or, as the poet Wordsworth said, intimations of immortality.

We know this much: this is yet another time to be gentle with ourselves. It is an important step to take, but in our own time and in our own way.

Resource Section

Helpful Books

As human beings we communicate primarily through the spoken word we use in much of our daily life. But we also encounter the utility and purposefulness of language in the written word. For some their bible is the truest comfort; for some poetry or the stories of great authors. For some reading helps them escape the daily tensions and the ups and downs of modern living. We read because we are social animals and we need the mental and spiritual nourishment that inspiring and insightful words can provide. In the written word we search our imaginations to reach the author on some common ground of understanding and empathy. It is as if our very beings call us to this activity.

In our grieving too, reading can play an important role. We read of hope and the resiliency of the human spirit. We read about practical ways to cope with what has happened in our lives. And we read of a better time coming, a brighter tomorrow, somewhere beyond this day. The following are a small sample of volumes on the grieving process that may offer the unique comfort of the healing word.

Experiencing Grief by H. Norman Wright
Though written from a Christian perspective the author is never pious or proselytizing but rather adept at being present with the reader through the tumult of personal grief, the expectations of the future and eventual hope of a new life. Author of over seventy books, Norman Wright walks with the reader through the common emotions of grief and remains to offer comfort, insight, and counsel in a highly readable and helpful volume.

One More Day by Mitch Albom
The acclaimed author of the bestselling and , gives us a fictional account of a man, Chick Benetto, confronting the gravest crisis of his life when he stumbles back into the house where he grew up. There his mother, dead eight years, is alive again, as if she never died. It is Chick's chance to spend one more day with his mother. What will he say and do? How will he act? A fascinating journey that reaches into our grief and finds the lessons of life hiding behind death.

Tear Soup by Pat Schweibert and Chuck DeKlyen
A creative volume for kids and adults, understands that our grieving is much like the making of soup: individual, personal, taken in slowly and with our senses alive to the experience. It is a recipe that adeptly and sweetly illumines our humanity. Pat Schweibert, founder of Grief Watch, has created with her co-author and illustrator a book many grief counselors have chosen to use with grieving people of all ages. A richly illustrated story that touches the heart and teaches some essential lessons about human loss.

Resource Section

Helpful Books

Healing After Loss: Daily Meditations for Walking Through Grief
by Martha Whitmore Hickman
  In its fortieth printing the effervescent Martha Whitmore Hickman has created a daily meditation guide as a collection of meaningful quotations and pulling from her own experience of the loss of her seventeen year old daughter after falling from a horse. Mrs. Hickman, born in 1925, is the author of 28 books and has parlayed her love for life and life's sacred moments into books for all ages and subject matter.

Kayak Morning by Roger Rosenblatt
  Award winning essayist, playwright, novelist and professor of English Literature and Writing, Roger Rosenblatt, lost his grown daughter to an undiagnosed heart condition. She was a wife and mother of young children. Roger and his wife moved in with the family after their daughter's death. The resulting book was , which described with the poet's eye those difficult and beautiful times as a part of a "new" family. This volume meditates on the experience of grief itself and grieving in general. The same grasp of the almost mystical details of life informs every page of Mr. Rosenblatt's writing.

Love is Stronger than Death by Peter Kreeft
  Dr. Kreeft, a professor of Philosophy at Boston College and prolific author, uses the disciplines of philosophy, literature, mythology, and religion to demystify death and make an eloquent case for death as a true beginning. Beautifully insightful, Kreeft examines the meaning of death in cultures and in hearts. Though the volume is deeply penetrating, this author of over sixty-five books knows how to make the subtleties of a subject accessible to the common reader. This highly perceptive and poetic treatise on death touches on the sacred qualities of our greatest transition.

The Grief Recovery Handbook by John W. James and Russell Freidman
  The authors are founders of the Grief Recovery Institute and for over thirty years they have conducted seminars and certification programs in the area of grief recovery. As in the first edition, their latest version is an exhaustive resource of insight discussing the many and varied issues grieving people encounter from myths concerning grief to confusion over the stages one may experience. This is a magnificent resource from two gentlemen who have worked with thousands of those in the midst of sorrow and loss.

Helpful Organizations and Websites

There are many organizations dedicated to helping people and groups suffering from loss and living in grief. To tap into the resources and fellowship offered from others is in itself a healing act, for it is a recognition that we are not alone, that there is indeed a common ground of humanity that can be of great comfort in difficult times. Today, most of the helpful organizations are easily available online, with internet websites that offer immediate information and resources. The following are but a few of those resources available.

The Grief Recovery Institute

An internationally recognized authority on grief recovery, with training programs, a Grief Recovery Handbook, as well as outreach, certification and community education programs.

Tel. (800) 334-7606 (toll free)
Website: www.griefrecoverymethod.com
E-mail: cacontact@grief.net

The National Hospice and Palliative Care Organization (NHPCO)

The largest non-profit membership organization representing hospice and palliative care programs and professionals in the United States. The organization is committed to improving end of life care and expanding access to hospice care with the goal of profoundly enhancing the quality of life for people dying in America and their loved ones.

Tel. (703) 837-1500
Website: www.nhpco.org
E-mail: nhpco info@nhpco.org

GriefNet

Griefnet is an Internet community of persons dealing with grief, death and major loss. Griefnet operates as a non-profit organization and also operates a companion site, KIDSAID. KIDSAID provides a safe, on line place for kids and their parents to find information and ask questions concerning loss and grief.

Website: www.GriefNet.org
Website: www.KIDSAID.com
E-mail: cendra@griefnet.org

Helpful Organizations and Websites

KinderMourn
In addition to servicing the special needs of bereaved parents, KinderMourn assists children who are grieving the death of a family member or friend. KinderMourn's professional grief facilitators are also provide individual and group counseling.
Tel. (704) 376-2580
    Website: www.kindermourn.org
    E-mail: info@kindermourn.org

The Compassionate Friends
A non-profit self help support organization designed to assist families in the positive resolution of grief following the death of a child and to provide information to help others be supportive.
    Tel. (630) 990-0010
    Website: www.compassionatefriends.org
    E-mail available on website

SHARE Pregnancy and Infant Loss Support, Inc.
The mission of SHARE Pregnancy and Infant Loss Support, Inc. is to serve those who have been touched by the death of a baby through early pregnancy loss, stillbirth, or in the first few months of life. The web site offers a packet of grief literature, information on local chapters, bimonthly newsletter, and resources.
    Tel. (800) 821-6819 (toll free)
    Website: www.nationalshareoffice.com
    E-mail available on website

National SUID/SID Resource Center
NSRC provides information services and technical assistance on sudden unexpected infant death (SUID), sudden infant death syndrome (SIDS) and related topics. The mission is to promote understanding of SUID/SIDS and provide comfort to those affected by SUID/SIDS through information sharing.
    Tel. (239) 431-5425
    Website: www.sidscenter.org
    E-mail: info@sidscenter.org

Survivors of Suicide
SOS is a bereavement support and information division of the American Association of Suicidology, a not-for-profit organization that is dedicated to the understanding and prevention of suicide.
    Tel. (202) 237-2280
    Website: www.survivorsofsuicide.com

Resource Section

Helpful Organizations and Websites

No Greater Love
No Greater Love (NGL) is a non-profit, humanitarian, patriotic organization dedicated to providing annual programs of remembrance, friendship and care for families who lost a loved one in the service of our country or by an act of terrorism. The emotional support system has been especially devoted to children who have lost a parent in service to our country.
    Tel. (855) 375-6453 (toll free)
    Website: www.nglfoundation.org
    E-mail: nogreaterlovefoundation@gmail.com

Renew: Center for Personal Recovery
Specialists in Crisis management for Schools and other Organizations. Renew offers services for individuals, families and organizations experiencing any kind of trauma or loss. Educational resources and workshops available.
    Tel. (850) 806-6236
    Website: www.renew.net
    E-mail: renewctr@gmail.com

The National Organization of Parents of Murdered Children
POMC is a national helping organization which is specifically for the survivors of homicide victims and which follows up with supportive family services after the murder of a family member or friend.
    Tel. (888) 818-POMC (toll free)
    Website: www.pomc.com
    E-mail: natlpmoc@aol.com

The Funeral Service Education Foundation
This division of the National Funeral Directors Association has information and resources on bereavement issues as well as other grief related materials.
    Tel. (800) 228-6332 (toll free)
    Website: www.nfda.org
    E-mail: nfda@nfda.org

WidowNet
An Internet information and self-help resource for, and by, widows and widowers. Topics covered include grief, bereavement, recovery and other information helpful to widows and widowers.
    Website: www.WidowNet.org
    E-mail: WidowNet@yahoogroups.com

Notes

The Way of Hope: A Thank You

May we take this space to thank you, for we know that in the days and weeks that have passed you have demonstrated to those around you the redeeming qualities of bearing one's grief with honesty and grace. You have helped someone without knowing it, someone who was watching as you trudged through your sorrow, deeply hurt, but marching forward to bring a measure of the love you have known in your life to others in need of it. Your witness calls to mind the famous lines of Robert Browning:

> *I walked a mile with Pleasure;*
> *She chattered all the way.*
> *But left me none the wiser*
> *For all she had to say.*
> *I walked a mile with Sorrow*
> *And ne'er a word said she;*
> *But oh, the things I learned from her*
> *When Sorrow walked with me!*

You have also thanked others for their care and concern for you in your difficult times. You have shown the worth of gratitude by employing it in your own life. We thank you for this expression as we also thank those who made this keepsake volume available. They chose this volume desiring to bring to you a measure of comfort, consolation and hope. It is our desire also that this is what our volume will mean to you in the months and years to come. Thank you for enduring your burdens as you have, and thereby demonstrating to others that it can be done and that there is something beyond the day's woe and the night's tears. Thank you for helping to show us all the way... the way of hope.